BECOMING ANNIE

THE BIOGRAPHY OF A CURIOUS WOMAN

DAWN BATES

DAWN PUBLISHING

CONTENTS

Foreword	vii
Gratitude	ix
1. Becoming Informed	1
2. Becoming Resilient	5
3. Becoming Aware	13
4. Becoming Anorexic	19
5. Becoming Daddy's Girl	27
6. Becoming Attractive	33
7. Dear Annie	39
8. Becoming Annie	43
9. Becoming Nurse Annie	47
10. Becoming Parents	53
11. Becoming Exhausted	63
12. Becoming Managerial	71
13. Becoming a Master	83
14. Becoming Inspired	91
15. Snapshots of Life	103
16. Becoming Smarter	109
17. Becoming CEO	115
18. Becoming Magical	121
19. Becoming a Philanthropist	131
20. Becoming Innovative	137
21. Becoming Audacious	145
22. Becoming Wiser	153
23. Becoming Reflective	161
Learn more about Annie	165
Author Profile	167

*To my grandmothers
Irena Volkova and Mary Montgomery
For bravely modelling how pioneering women can use their purpose and passion to intentionally rise above their circumstance in ways which positively impact the world around them.*

© 2020 Dawn Bates

Published by Dawn Publishing
www.dawnbates.com
The moral right of the author has been asserted.

For quantity sales or media enquiries, please contact the publisher at the website address above.

Cataloguing-in-Publication entry is available from the British Library.

ISBN: 978-0-9957322-6-1 (paperback)
978-0-9957322-7-8 (ebook)

Book cover design – Miladinka Milic

All rights reserved. No part of this book may be reproduced, stored in a retrieval system, communicated or transmitted in any form or by means without written permission. All inquiries should be made to the publisher at the above address.

Disclaimer: The material in this publication is of the nature of general comment only and does not represent professional advice. It is not intended to provide specific guidance for particular circumstances and should not be relied on as the basis for any decision to take action or not to take action on any matters which it covers.

Foreword

Women of today are forging a new path for themselves, no longer needing to be men in a man's world, and that in part is due to women like Annie Gibbins.

I met Annie years ago at a business maximiser group called Troublemakers. We were two edgy women who were willing to be uncomfortable to take their businesses to the next level and beyond.

By opening ourselves up to peer review and diving deep into other versions of bold growth goals designed to explore, unpack and explode our true potential, we grew together.

I sat next to Annie and watched her brainstorm the launch of her mentoring business she called Lipstick Consulting. This was only the beginning, not just of our businesses, but of a deep friendship.

Upon meeting Annie, I was immediately impressed by her resilience, her unbelievable coping skills and her ability to cut through to what is important, alongside her huge capacity for caring for others.

Over the years I have watched her achieve a great many things with her incredible strength, determination, endless energy and boundless curiosity.

Becoming Annie reflects her achievements at home, as a nurse, as a mum, a mentor, a philanthropist and as the CEO of Glaucoma Australia.

Annie is aspirational, her story inspirational and this book is a must-read for any person juggling a multitude of tasks, especially women. She is a shining example of how you can achieve great success even when you are pulled in a million directions and how one person can make such an enormous difference to those around them.

The launch of her women's mentoring and coaching business, called Lipstick Consulting, which was the beginning of her vision to be a part of creating positive change in the world continues to support, encourage and develop women into their fullest potential, and for that I am truly proud to know her.

I congratulate Annie on this book and just know that she will continue to change the world with every new endeavour she takes on.

Anthea Leonard
Founder, Creative and Managing Director of Sweet Art.
Cake Artistry, Corporate & Private Event Design & Production.
Australia's Premier Cake Design Company, the preferred choice for A list celebrities around the world.
www.sweetart.com.au

Gratitude

I'd like to express my deepest appreciation to my biographer Dawn Bates who miraculously unpacked 50 years of my crazy life journey and crafted my story to share with the love and grace of a soul sister. It required a strong cocktail of endless chatter, belly laughs and tears streaming down our faces but resulted in my tale being stripped bare and a grateful heart towards all that I love and am yet to experience and relish.

To my loving husband James, I'm so glad I let that hunky young man drive me home age 17 as after 35 years together I still feel blessed every day to be your wife. Navigating the journey of life with you has certainly been a crazy unorthodox ride so it's a good thing we both like rollercoasters! I am grateful for your friendly nature, engaging personality, generous spirit and quirky personality as you bring abundant joy, love and happiness into my heart and into our family. Thank you for being the great man you are, you complement me in every way.

To my beautiful children Caleb, Daniel, Samuel, Hannah and Chelsea, daughters in-law Bethany and Alice and granddaughter Lizzie, you are a constant ray of sunshine in my life and my prayer is that you will all be happy, healthy and successful in your own ways, on you own terms.

To my dear friends who listen to my endless chatter as we hike mountains and beaches, enjoy coffee shops, drinking champagne and have fun adventures – I love each and every one of you. xo

To Ilda Wade, thank you for being my soul sister in every sense of the word.

To Stephen De Sede, thank you for steering my path towards my true purpose and passion.

To Melanie Kell, thank you for honouring my gifts, talents and expertise.

Annie xoxox

Dream big and believe that all things are possible

Chapter One

BECOMING INFORMED

Growing up by the ocean in the beautiful relaxed surfer haven of Manly, right on Sydney Harbour, Anne-Marie Montgomery was blessed with a playground most people can only dream of.

With endless bush trails and ocean walks, and the secret waterfalls of Collins Flat Beach, there is no wonder the woman you are about to discover has a deep and curious nature. Life sounds idyllic, especially when you consider the golden sandy beaches, turquoise water and a horseshoe bay Anne-Marie had at her disposal.

With a playful nature, a strong sense of knowing what she wanted and did not want to do in life, combined with what some would call a rebellious streak, the name Anne-Marie would soon become a thing of the past; and the vivacious and effervescent Annie would burst onto the scene.

Now it would be easy to think that life has been smooth sailing, full of endless praise and support for the woman you are about to encounter, and whilst that is true to a point, a real success isn't one of glitter balls and sparkles all the time.

For those who meet the woman Anne-Marie has become today, it would be hard to imagine in many ways that her life has been anything other than idyllic; but therein lies the grace and beauty of the woman now known as Annie.

Yes, Annie is positive; yes, she has incredible energy that radiates from deep within her; yes, her strength and vision is what makes her a powerhouse of a woman. But as with all successful people, there is a story of grit, challenges and heartache along the way...

Because just like every single person on the planet, successful people, including Annie, are simply human beings, living life the only way they know how; by being themselves in their own way, day by day, hour by hour, and sometimes, minute by excruciating minute.

Now for some people it would be easy to judge and say, "Oh it's easy for her, her daddy had his own business and her mum was a stay at home mum." But this does not make Annie, or anyone else, exempt from the trials and tribulations of discovering who they are, what their place is in the world and what their journey actually means for them.

Childhood and the teenage years for everyone can be fraught with uncertainty, wanting to fit in, a deep desire to please parents and teachers alike. It is a minefield of hormones and emotions that do not make sense to anyone, least of all the person experiencing them.

Parents are often heard saying they don't understand their children, some wonder where they went wrong, whilst many have long forgotten, in the whirlwind and suppression of their own struggles, just how challenging it is to navigate the stormy waters of high school, raging hormones, body image and clothing disasters, all finished off with a great big dose of day dreaming and dreams of the future.

As adults we expect teenagers to know what they are going to be doing with their lives by the time it comes to take those all-important career exams at the age of 16 and 17. We want them to have their careers all figured out, following in the family footsteps, or avoiding them at all costs, whilst many adults still have no idea at the age of 35, 45 and then crash and burn at age 55.

With the onslaught of urges, insecurities and more often than not the high school bullies, living the teenage dream is not all it is cracked up to be.

The story you are about to read may be the story of an incredibly successful woman, a woman who has risen in the ranks of the Australian medical world, and it is a story which will trigger other women in a whole myriad of ways, but it is also the story of a young woman in her fifties who still has a heart-warming crush on her high school sweetheart, a loving mother who will do whatever it takes to provide the best for her children, and it is the story of a loving friend who cares deeply and loyally, whilst also bringing out the best in everyone.

Annie is a woman who has lived an extraordinary life, because she herself is extraordinary; and whilst we may imagine this word to mean there is nothing ordinary about her, it is her very ordinary desire to be a kind and loving person which makes her one of the most ordinary, *and* unforgettable, women you will ever read about.

You will be taken on a journey through the life of a woman who has more curiosity than Alice in the land of wonder and when you close the book at the end, you will not only be impressed, inspired and ready to up your own game, diving deeper into what is possible for yourself, but you will be left with a feeling of sadness that the tale has come to an end, coupled with joy for having been witness to the greatness as it unfolds.

Annie is a woman who is always expanding her capacity for greatness, and whilst most women of her calendar age would be slowing down, Annie is still bursting with energy and excitement of what is truly possible, delighting in *What's next?* and in her own high speed words and infectious giggle, declares, "I am like a fine wine, I get better with age."

So, without further ado, allow me to introduce you to the one and only Mrs Annie Gibbins.

Everyone's a little quirky, aren't they?

Chapter Two
BECOMING RESILIENT

Imagine yourself all excited and full of life, training hard in the sport of your choice. You have big dreams, have this smile on your face, knowing you are destined for greatness. You see your name in lights, on billboards around the world, and there you are centre stage captivating every audience you meet.

The smile on your face has given your facial muscles the best workout possible, so much so your face aches in the best possible way. You bow to your audience, who are raising the roof with their thundering applause, your heart overflowing with joy, not quite believing this is all possible, but going with it anyway.

You know you are here to change the world; this belief in yourself lights you up in each and every moment; and it shows. You are radiant, your eyes sparkling, and you are so enthusiastic you've almost reached the point of excitement where only dogs can hear your voice.

And then that moment is shattered, and the people you love most in the world are the ones responsible.

Growing up in a home, the youngest of three children, Annie was on the receiving end of daily taunts and abusive actions by her eldest brother. Now whilst this may seem the normal sibling rivalry, sometimes the relentless bullying and verbal taunts which become the norm, are the start of what will become a living nightmare that will last a lifetime, leaving untold damage in its wake; and it all started with one soul destroying conversation with her mother.

With dreams of being a world-famous ballerina, Annie trained like her life depended on it. Every day was ballet day, but Friday nights, they were the highlight of the week!

Eagerly gathering her things, tutu and ballet cardigan at the ready, hair tightly up in a bun, and her baby pink tights underneath the soft pink body, it was time to shine like the radiant star on a global stage that she would one day become.

Eight years old and about to take on the world of ballet, ready to take to the stage at any moment, joy bursting from every part of her, Annie was ready.

The world would see her dance, applaud her in gratitude for her awe-inspiring talent and for telling the most beautiful love stories in the most graceful and silent of ways.

She was going to be a famous ballerina just like her Russian born Aunt Anna Volkova; that was until the moment she excitedly told her grandma, "I'm going to be a famous ballerina just like Auntie Ania." And instead of encouragement and dream building, her grandmother delivered the words which reverberated and shattered this dream into a thousand tiny pieces.

Feeling the anger rise up within her, tears falling down her face, Annie went to her mother. She would surely be as equally shocked and upset at her grandma's response.

"You'll never believe what Mama[1] said to me! She even made me cry! She said that I will never be a world-famous ballerina like Aunt Ania. She told me I have legs like an elephant!"

But what Annie heard next, would be equally devastating, and lay the foundations of years of self-doubt.

"Darling, Mama is right. You will not be a world-famous ballerina. You don't have legs like an elephant... but you do have a lot of puppy fat. You don't have the body to be a ballerina." Delivered in a soothing way, graced by the word "Darling" at the beginning of the sentence, as if that would make it less painful to hear, Annie's mother sealed the fate on a life of dance.

Feeling fragile, fat and ugly, dreams crushed right there in front of her, by the very person who should have been there to turn fears and doubts into courage and confidence, Annie couldn't believe her own mother could say such a thing.

Alchemising the strength and determination, the foundation of resilience in this young girl, Annie returned to her ballet class the following week to watch, witness and explore her future with ballet through this new lens.

With eyes now wide open, she suddenly started to notice all the skinny girls in the front row twirling around effortlessly.

Ballet had never been effortless for Annie. Seeds of doubt started to germinate. Asking her ballet teacher if she could stand in the front row during class, she was met with the response of, "No, not this time. Maybe another time."

Mind whirring, fears rising and interpretation inception, this 'No' became a confirmation of what her mother and grandmother had been telling her.

She was an elephant. She had fat legs. She was fat, puppy fat or not, it still had the word fat at the end of the phrase; and for a young prepubescent girl, using the word fat anywhere in a sentence is never a good idea.

Hearing her mother telling her she had weight issues even as a baby, didn't help Annie's fragile self-esteem.

Deciding never to go to ballet ever again, having formed the opinion that she was a terrible dancer, and definitely too fat to belong in a room of dancers, Annie went home and announced that she was taking up swimming instead.

With swimming her body would be hidden underneath the water, so no one would see her 'fat legs, her fat body and the clumsiness of an elephant'.

Taking to the water and training every Saturday with a midweek session thrown in for good measure, Annie was not only about to get her asthma under control, to a point, but she would use her determination to develop strong arms and shoulders; something which would hold her in good stead in the coming years.

As with most families, there are just some things which do not stay secret for very long. Annie's family is no different, and soon those devastating words would become known as the reason why Annie had chosen to stop going to ballet.

When her teenage brothers got wind of what Mama and her mother had said, it was time for them to step into the stereotypical big brother 'taunt and tease' mode of operandi. This would become their advantage; their latest entertainment and they would create endless moments of comedy from the situation.

With the new nickname 'Fatty' fixed firmly in their minds, Annie's brothers would spend the following years using Annie as their toy of shame, no matter how much she cried and begged her mother to make them stop. They wouldn't stop, they didn't want to. Why would they when she was the fat baby of the family who provided hours of entertainment for them?

'Boys will be boys', 'stop crying and ignore them' and 'your puppy fat will go soon my darling' would be the phrases Annie, as well as countless other young girls around the world, would hear for the entire time the 'school boy teasing' continued.

Friends at school were disapproved of on a regular basis, especially if the mother of said friends happened to be a career woman. Believing firmly in the notion that any woman who chose to get married and have children should stay at home in their early years, Annie's mother made it increasingly difficult for Annie to bring friends home from school.

Friends were 'forced' upon Annie by her mother, the ones she deemed worthy of befriending her daughter. Did they come from a good family? Were their parents professional. If so, then they were acceptable. Natalie, Annie's best friend from school, was the daughter of a TV producer's assistant and Katie Louise's father owned a pub, so Heidi was the preferred friend as her dad was the local doctor.

After being taken away by ambulance from the school cross country carnival, sports were avoided to prevent life threatening asthma attacks and Annie chose to look elsewhere for after school activities.

With the school musical coming up, and excitement building, Annie pictured herself on stage once more. Lights, make-up, outfits, an audience mesmerised by the performance, the thunderous round of applause and a standing ovation at the end full of gratitude, yep! The school musical was her opportunity to get on stage. Okay, so it wouldn't be twirling in a tutu and being thrown gracefully in the air by strong men in tights, but the school musical gave Annie hope.

That was until her mother killed yet another dream due a strong dislike of the school's Music Director, combined with yet more fear and declarations of hospitals and imminent death. "Singing and dancing will put pressure on your lungs" and "It could kill you" came before a flat-out refusal to allow Annie to take part.

Another hope dashed, along with all the other dreams shattered and scattered across the floor. Anne-Marie – being Annie, though – was not going to allow this to dampen her spirit or dim her radiance. With each knock-back, another brick in the wall of determination would be placed firmly into position. The more her mother knocked her, the more her father encouraged her to consider pharmacy as a career. One did not equal the other, nor did they have any connection.

Mr Montgomery was incredibly focused on providing for his family to really notice the depth of bullying, and it would be this focus which he would pass onto his only daughter by the truck load. The more Annie's dreams were being chipped away at, the more Mr Montgomery was dreaming of his beautiful daughter, who he doted on, working alongside him in the family business.

In moments when her mother became more and more frustrated with Annie, she would shout "I never wanted a girl, girls are trouble", further destroying any self-belief which remained within this young girl, who just wanted to dance, swim and be happy. Coupled with a father who spent long hours at the pharmacy and submerged in the running of the business, Annie felt more and more alone.

Things got decidedly worse whenever her mother would go in search of something in particular like money in her wallet or an Easter egg in a bowl. If she couldn't find it, out would come the belt, a common practice for many families during this time, but it still didn't make it any easier knowing others also had the 'belt taken to them'.

Hearing the sound of the belt buckle, the swish of the leather, the whisper of the air as the belt came whooshing down across the bare flesh of either Annie's or her elder brothers, the fear would grip Annie tightly.

The whippings would only stop when Annie confessed, even if she wasn't to blame for the thing going missing. Considering her brothers were three and six years older than her, she has resigned herself to the theory 'it was better to just admit to taking whatever it was instead of having the whippings continue'.

Life was not pleasant, and it was only about to get a whole lot worse.

---

1. Mama – the name Annie uses for Grandma

Every girl has a princess inside of her

Chapter Three
BECOMING AWARE

Her relationship with her dad, the man who worked tirelessly building the family business, was strong, even though time with him was scarce. Leader, protector and provider for his family, served by a wife who served his family, he was the rock in Annie's world. The safe haven she would seek out in those moments of need, and the man she wanted to please in many ways. He was her dad, and the mix of awe and love she had for him, made her want to make him proud.

Living in Manly, a suburb named by Captain Arthur Philips in acknowledgement of the Aboriginal people who lived there when he arrived, meant a certain set of standards to behold. With a history of multiculturalism, sub-tropical climate and plenty of surfer action, Manly was a town with a great number of tourists. With 'el fresco' dining around The Corso, the wharf and cheaper food and drink stands by the ferry terminal, this small cove had its fair share of day trippers coming and going, bringing new faces every day.

It wasn't just the surfers and golden sandy beaches that put Manly on the map though, it was the Manly-Warringah Sea Eagles, the local rugby league heroes. It is no big secret that rugby league is a pretty big deal in Australia, so having a local team which has been appearing in the grand finals since the 1950s, meant crowds of people wanting to rub shoulders with their sporting heroes would flock to the seaside suburb.

Providing a life for his family in the Northern Beaches area of Sydney, Australia not only meant that Annie's dad had chosen one of the more affluent areas of Australia to raise a family, but it also meant he worked longer hours than most men to provide for his family. The old adage of 'One does not come without the other' rings true now as it did back in the 1960s and 70s.

Growing up so close to the ocean, sailing was one of her dad's favourite past times. Always happy serving a customer in the pharmacy, an occasional weekend afternoon sailing on Middle Harbour was a luxury but his happy place. It was something that would light up his kind face and bring peace to his heart. His love of sailing didn't just play out along the coast, he would take his family sailing and fishing everyday whilst on the annual family holiday down by the Bellingen River, near Coffs Harbour.

Surrounded by the Dorrigo National Park, with its beautiful waterfalls, rock pools and trails, the family holidays brought a lot of fun to Annie's life. Playing in the river, fishing on the banks, and exploring all the natural beauty by day, and falling asleep in the cabin at night, listening to her parents chatting away with their friends, Annie had a huge amount of joy to counter balance the upsets she experienced.

At the age of 10 when her best friend Louise asked her to go to the ABBA concert with her to celebrate her birthday. How could a 10-year-old girl be anything less than thrilled? A pop concert with a bestie and her mum aged 10! Excited just didn't cover it! With the build up to the concert, it was all the girls could talk about, planning outfits, glitter at the ready the girls danced and sang their hearts out all night, loving absolutely every moment of it.

The time spent with her grandmothers allowed Annie to be loved and spoilt by two very different women from very different worlds, both of fierce strength and courage. This resilience and determination from both grandmothers not only passed on through the bloodline, a bloodline which reached as far as Russia and Germany, but also in the stories shared in the endless conversations on the special days Annie would enjoy with each.

With regular days out by bus with her grandma to see horse shows and go bargain hunting, treats of a Russian Easter with her mama, including the compulsory vodka shots of every Russian celebration; and days out with her grandad to the club for lunch, Annie enjoyed the attention of her grandparents, and the constant chatter about everything and anything. These conversations would be part of the treasure trove of memories she would hold dear to her heart long after they had ended and would make a lot more sense later in Annie's life.

Whilst the family business provided a comfortable life, it also brought with it a danger that would leave Annie feeling incredibly nervous and 'freaked out' for the best part of a year.

One morning, aged 10, Annie woke up to find out one of her brothers was missing, whilst the family had all been sleeping, and from the bedroom right next to Annie's; more fuel to add onto the simmering firing of fear and nervousness Annie felt on a deep level.

Thoughts that her brother had gone surfing were erased when a handwritten note was found. It was the only clue they would find and that was sketchy at best, especially as it was written in her brothers handwriting. The note read 'I've got the kid' which was not what a disgruntled teenager who was annoyed with his parents would leave if her had gone off for a couple of days of surfing.

Had he written it himself? Did he want to worry his parents for some kind of payback? Had he been made to write the note under duress, and if so, what kind of duress? Was he taken for ransom? Did they want money or drugs? What was required to get him back? Where was he? Who had him?

With the police informed and adult conversations being held, the hunt for her brother started. With parents caught up in the frenzy of finding her brother, Annie was left alone to deal with her own emotions and thought processes. No information was provided, and she was told to stay out of the way.

Three days after the kidnapping, her brother broke free of the house he was being kept in Avalon and ran for the beach. When he saw a bus approaching, he jumped in front of it and the driver stopped and allowed him to board. With a ride to the police station sorted, and a return to the family home, everything would appear to be back to normal. That is until the next day the Manly Daily ran an article in the paper about how her brother had been found.

Annie wanted answers to her questions and the questions her friends at school kept asking. Instead of being asked to sit down and having a conversation about all that was happening, her parents told her to stop being nosey and under no uncertain terms was she to discuss it with anyone else. This had nothing to do with anyone else, it was a private family matter.

So why then had the Manly Daily run the story if this was a private family matter, and how on earth did they find out?

She had been told not to ask questions or talk about it, hushed up and told to be quiet. With the quiet, the number of questions grew and all were left unanswered.

The questions would circulate around in Annie's mind for months. "How did the paper get the story? Did the police give it to them? Why were her parents not pressing charges? Were they being threatened? If so, with what? Why did they just want it all to go away? Surely someone must be held accountable for what they had done!

So many questions swimming around in her head, and the pressure mounting, the fear silently creeping up behind her like a secret assassin. Annie felt alone, confused and afraid, and still no one was asking her how she was feeling about this whole scenario; not even her dad, her safe haven.

What had felt like a really safe home, in a safe neighbourhood had now become a place of fear, especially when her parents started deadbolting doors and windows, and turning the property into a mini Fort Knox. Her parents were creating a prison in her own home.

Walking to and from school, especially when alone, Annie would keep looking around on high alert. Was there someone lying in wait? Where were the bad guys? Were they coming for her next? Was it safe to walk this path? Should she change the routes to school each day? Or just stick to the same route, just in case something did happen, and people had no idea where to start looking for her?

The anxiety was building. Her concentration and studies were getting worse, and so were her eating habits. A loss of appetite caused by the anxiety of having no answers to her questions, not having someone to talk about her brothers disappearance, and the still lingering poor body image, is there any wonder Annie needed to find a way of taking back some of the control she felt she was losing on a deeper subconscious level.

As with all of us who go through a trauma, there is an in built need to find 'an out', a desire to regain the control we never knew we had until it was gone; like the breath we are holding in a moment of shock that sends us light headed and crashing to the floor. There were many things Annie needed. A hug from her parents, answers to her endless questions and words of reassurance, would have nourished part of it, but the increased focus on safety at home and on the streets, the beaches where she and her friends had played, all now masked by the fear of being next in line. Had it triggered memories of young Graeme Thorne who had gone missing and been found murdered just a few streets from where Annie had grown up? Or was it simply because with everything else being taken away from her, she needed to feel in control.

There were lots of needs in Annie's life during this time, and with the comments from her grandmother and mother about her weight still lingering in her mind, she wanted to lose weight, needed to lose weight. She needed to hold *it* all together whatever *it* was, and with the growing feelings of not being important, unwanted by her mother because she was a girl, being a child asking questions she had no right in asking, Annie began to take control of everything she was experiencing in the only way she knew how.

If you don't love yourself, why would anyone else?

Chapter Four
BECOMING ANOREXIC

With the constant name calling at home by her brothers, the whippings and criticism by her mother, and dreams shattered on the floor, Annie lost all the idealistic desires she'd once had.

Annie's oldest brother took the bullying to a whole other level when he chose to sexually assault her. First, he started taking inappropriate photos with his new camera, intimidating Annie and threatening her, before going on to rape her. Annie didn't tell her mother what had happened, she couldn't; and even if she did, her mother already thought of her as a liar, so what would be the point?

With threats of 'or else' and of killing her if she told anyone, combined with shaming her by showing everyone her 'fat slut' pictures, her brother was able to get away with it all. Plus, he had 'all the proof' he needed that she had 'asked for it'. Annie's depth of loneliness, fear and shame alchemised into a strength that would stand her in great stead later in life, she just didn't know it yet, but it played out every single day she lived at home with her brother. Having to face him day in and day out took huge amounts of courage, and although she had told her mum she didn't want to be alone with her brother as he was rough and mean, her mum dismissed her.

And would her mother believe her? Could any mother believe this would happen in her own family? Brother raping sister, the stuff of horror movies, something that happened to 'other people', hard to believe it could happen at all, let alone in your own family. She had sacrificed so much of herself to be the perfect wife and mother, carefully choosing the friends her children had, creating an idyllic life in which to raise a family, giving her family her own version of total devotion, as well as battling her own internal demons and disappointments. No, this was just something that could not happen, or would not have happened, in her family; but she wouldn't get to find out, not yet anyway.

This latest blow to Annie, and her mother, created an even bigger divide between the two of them. Unable to speak with her parents about it, there was no one to help her process what had just happened. She felt 100% alone. She felt scared. And not forgetting the insults from her brother that she was a 'fat slut', the light within Annie only felt like a flicker in a vast mine of darkness, but in reality, it couldn't have been further from the truth.

As seen the world over, it only takes a spark to light up the night sky, and with the bush fires of Australia being a regular occurrence, it seemed Annie has inherited a spark that could not and would not be extinguished.

Annie knew things were going to get better. They always did, and with a deep faith in God, Annie knew she was loved, it said so in the Bible, even if it didn't feel like it at times. She had to believe she was loved by someone other than her dad, a love she never questioned.

Brownies was the weekly boost of fun Annie needed, and with an ever-increasing collection of badges, Annie and the other Brownies would go on to join the Girl Guides as well as move up into the new world of high school. A daunting move for some, but not for Annie and her best friend Natalie. They were super excited to be starting with their other friends.

As the first day of high school arrived the best friends started making new friends together, but by the end of the first week, Annie noticed Natalie had started to become distant and was beginning to spend all of her time with some of the other new girls. Sitting with her new friends at lunch, Natalie started to avoid Annie whenever she got the chance.

Now being the younger sister of two older brothers, Annie had learnt to stand up to herself, even if she did find it difficult to escape the taunts and teasing at home. After a few days of being avoided, the desire to know why got the better of Annie, and with courage gained and the question locked and loaded, Annie confronted her best friend with "Can I sit with you and your new friends? We are best friends."

Natalie's response was to be yet another crushing blow to Annie's self-esteem, "Actually no, my new friendship group is called 'The Models,' and you don't look like a model, so you can't sit with us. They're gorgeous, they're skinny, and you're just… not."

Fighting back tears, pushing the pain down inside, Annie's friendship and her confidence shattered right there in that moment. Her best friend had dumped her for The Models, the gorgeous and skinny girls she had only just met. Turning and walking away, mind spinning, heart breaking, Annie went to the bathroom and cried her heart out. Tears and emotions coming in waves, and not just about the devastating blow she had just received either; but from it all. All of the rejection, all of the insults, the name calling, being overlooked, and the loneliness.

A traumatising experience for any young girl to go through, and one in which the majority do go through at some point in their teenage years, but for Annie after everything she was experiencing at home, her father unaware due to the hours he worked, it became a downward spiral.

The thing is though, when you have a fierce determination like Annie has, only greatness can come from it all. She used these negative emotions to fuel her inner fire, and from that fire came a determination like no other, a determination that would grow and evolve with each new challenge she faced. Being a teenager with hormones raging, and the tools of life still developing, the determination to lose weight took Annie on a path which would impact her and her future as a mother in ways no one could have ever foretold.

Skipping meals, hiding food to put in the bin later, measuring body fat with the daily weigh-ins, standing in front of the mirror detesting her body, Annie was beginning to lose the weight. Week by week the hunger increased, but the desire to fit in and lose was stronger than the hunger pains. Annie soon began to learn how to nibble just enough of the right kind of foods to make sure she didn't pass out. She learnt how to avoid mealtimes and how to disguise the amount she wasn't eating.

Weigh-in by weigh-in Annie could start to see the results she wanted. At first her clothes started to look great. She started to mimic how 'The Models' wore their clothes, would spend hours looking at the fashion models to see how they dressed, because after weeks and weeks of starving herself, new clothes were needed. Instead of looking elfin and model like, she looked like a bag lady. Her hair started to lose its shine, but people were now complimenting her on how great she looked, and how much prettier she looked now she was losing the weight.

This fuelled the determination to continue hiding food, to continue with the Pinch Test, and slowly but surely Annie developed anorexia nervosa, an illness which can delay or stop a young girl from having her periods, as well as cause fertility problems later in life.

Even with all the comments on how great Annie looked, she was still not accepted into the group of girls called "The Models", nor did she wish to be. With many girls being fussy and picky about what they ate, combined with skipping meals, it took Annie a while to realise things were getting a little out of hand. The wake-up call she needed happened when she went to visit a friend who had been hospitalised with the same illness. Seeing just how bad things had got for her friend, and freaking out at the consequences of her current eating habits, Annie knew if she did not make the changes needed now, then it would be her in the hospital alongside others who were starving themselves to death.

With a stomach too small to cope with the new intake of food, Annie would start purging soon after she had eaten. With the acid levels inside her stomach all over the place, digesting the food was a slow and painful process. Jaw ache and an acrid taste in her mouth becoming a new sensation, Annie's transition from anorexia nervosa to bulimia was teaching her more about her relationship with her body and food than she realised at the time.

There was still a large amount of secrecy going on, hiding the food, hiding her body changes with clothes and only eating when it was safe to purge afterwards, Annie was dealing with this food journey all by herself.

During this year her parents bought the pharmacy where her dad had been a partner and her mother went from being at home to working full-time to support him. Trying to figure this out in her mind, Annie was processing a lot, far too much for a young girl to deal with by herself. Hugs with her dad would mean the world to her. She felt safe, protected, loved, but with the incredibly long hours he worked, there never seemed to be enough of them. Life at home was lonely and scary, so Annie would spend hours alone in her room reading and doing homework, or she would jump on her bike and head down to the beach, her happy place.

By the age of thirteen Annie had developed a taste in music which included listening to bands such as INXS, Cold Chisel, The Divinyls, Midnight Oil, Hoodoo Gurus, Split Enz and Skyhooks. A little on the soft rock side, and not quite in line with a love of ABBA Annie had developed years earlier.

The weeks rolled on by, Annie started to wag school; a combination of not wanting to be around the school bullies, the fear and anxiety brought on by the memories of the sexual abuse by her eldest brother, and her mother still unaware of what had happened, wagging school was the release she needed. It gave her the space to think, to be alone, to rebel and feel like there was some kind of control in her life.

Adding in the frustrations of not being able to take part in sports day, drama productions and seeing an unfairness to life, a 'rude and disrespectful' rebellious side was developing and would soon see Annie get kicked out of Girl Guides for something as simple as blowing a Hubba Bubba bubble in the line-up. The final straw for the Guide leader who'd had enough of Annie not following the rules, which if you asked Annie were pretty stupid rules anyway.

No one bothered to find out why this new attitude and set of rebellious behaviours had manifested, or why her image had changed so drastically. To the adults around her, she was just 'another typical teenager' who was navigating the hormones and finding herself, who had bouts of little to no respect for authority in amongst periods of being such a polite and lovely girl.

When Annie was 15, her brother was preparing to celebrate his 21st birthday. Things were still very strained between them, being in his company still filled her with fear and anxiety and the 'incident' had still not been discussed, but with his 21st birthday around the corner it was expected she be at the party.

With the party in full swing, everything was going well, until history repeated itself and Annie found herself at the mercy of two of her brother's friends. Could things get any worse? Is this what it meant to be a teenage girl? Really!?

Memories, fear and anxiety flooding back, combined with a whole new set of emotions, Annie experienced an overload of emotions and fear rising in so many different guises. No counselling, no support from anyone else, just Annie, finding her way and solving this puzzle of teenage life all by herself. A journey which would take her beyond her teenage years to complete, but this was one challenge she was determined to win, no matter how long it took.

Get rid of noise and clutter, it adds little value

Chapter Five
BECOMING DADDY'S GIRL

Hiding the eating disorders from her family, especially her dad who never knew the secrets weighing heavily on his daughter's soul, Annie continued to put on a brave face, faking it until she made it.

Having grandparents who were visiting regularly and the beach to escape to everyday helped with Annie's ability to process the traumas. The freedom of riding her bike around the local area with the smell of the ocean, wind in her hair might seem like a cliché to many, but it was as if Mother Nature was cleansing her as she rode along the trails and streets, preparing her for whatever was coming next; reminding her how wonderful it felt to be alive.

The days of lying on the beach, one of Annie's favourite past times allowed her to be still, to just simply be. Breathing in cleansed her and breathing out allowed her to let go. Listening but not listening to the waves, the gulls squawking up above, feeling the warmth and the brightness of the sun's fire on her face, hearing the waves fall away, basking in God's creation, a sense of peace would re-energise her. She didn't need any magic wand, because in these moments the magic was in the stillness, of truly gifting herself time to be, allowing herself to release all the fear and worries to God, the most powerful kind of prayer there is. A surrendering like no other.

These events Annie had been through, was going through, were all part of His Divine plan, and she had to trust that, she just had to. It was the belief that she was born for greater things, that the stage she dreamed of performing on was given to her for a reason. In these tender moments with God she allowed Him to truly shine His love on her; and she allowed herself to feel it, to receive it and to embrace it.

With her 'constant mood swings', not to mention the increase of confidence and the number of parties she was invited to, Annie's mum decided it was time to put her daughter on the pill. Was Annie really that moody? Or was it just another way to control and punish her daughter? Being told it was to prevent a teenage pregnancy didn't make sense because at the time of going on the pill, Annie hadn't even started her periods.

Weekly visits to church, being part of her church family, seeing a different set of friends boosted Annie's spirit even further. Learning about the different community projects and missionary work others were doing around the world gave Annie ideas of how others lived and made her so grateful for everything she did have, and grateful for all the things that hadn't happened to her. Things had been bad, but they were so much worse for so many others around the world and knowing this increased Annie's desire to be of service to others.

Weekly youth groups were held on a variety of subjects by the church and Annie would find them both interesting and enjoyable, developing her curious nature even more than ever.

Back at home, conversations with her dad had already started to tune in even more than ever to her future career choices. Not wanting to go into the day to day service side of the family pharmacy, Annie's interests and ambitions lay in becoming the manager, of running the business, creating something bigger and of 'doing the business'. It excited her and she could see herself being a great manager, and she knew she had it in her, a belief that would create not only a huge amount of success later in life, but a whole lot of humour to go with it.

With all the back and forth about what to do with her future career, Annie would receive another sign that working in the pharmacy full time was not what she wanted to do. With cash in the till, medication behind the counter, and the junkies needing their next fix meant the pharmacy was the ideal target for those in desperate need. The target of three armed robberies, these robberies would make yet more dents in the confidence levels, leave her with a fear of her dad dying, and no desire to join him running the family business.

Her dad knew she had been deeply shaken by the armed robberies and was as stubborn as a mule when it came to getting an idea out of her head, but that did not stop him wanting her to follow in his footsteps. He loved his daughter, wanted to spend more time with her, and would tell her how wonderful it would be working side by side in the family business serving customers all day. Annie didn't want to let her dad down, she loved him, wanted to make him proud of her, but working in the pharmacy all day? No, not something she wanted to do. She knew she had some serious thinking to do because there was no way she wanted to die at gun point with a junkie being the last person she saw, no way at all!

With the time fast approaching to choose the subjects for her HSC[1], Annie and her father had many disagreements. She knew he wanted the best for his daughter, he always had, but he had built the family business so he could pass it onto his children, to give them financial security, a place to work. He knew she had to study chemistry, and to go along with that he wanted her to take three units of economics. Knowing it wasn't all about the maths, but part of the much bigger global picture, and being in line with being in the medical and pharmaceutical profession, this seemed to fit Annie's grand plans and ideas as well as his own ideas.

His vision for the business included Annie, working with him, side by side, father and daughter together, talking, laughing and being together like they did on their Sunday sailing afternoons and the family holiday, but Annie had other ideas, much bigger ideas.

She knew going to work in a shop 'day in, day out' would drive her crazy, and as much as she loved her dad, and loved spending time with him, the thought of the same place, the same people, counting pills all day long, being surrounded by sickly customers, it was most definitely a no from Annie; in fact she dreaded the thought it.

During one of their many discussions, Annie told her dad, "You know Dad, one day, I will own the pharmacy."

To which he replied, "You don't have the aptitude to be a businesswoman. You're not good at maths, and anyway, it would be impossible to do it once you are a mother. You have seen it takes a lot of hours, and hours you won't have once you start having to look after your own children."

Stunned and disappointed by her father's view of her lack of potential, she looked at him. Knowing she could do it, whilst also believing dads knew best, Annie considered the possibility that maybe she should just get used to the idea of working in a shop, learning to like the idea of giving out pills to sick people all day; because like her dad said, "That's what women do – work in a shop, leaving the world of business to the men of the house."

Thinking through this dilemma was an emotional battle and she knew it just wasn't going to work. The more she thought about it, the more she disliked it. She just couldn't see herself there in the shop all day every day, waiting for the action to happen. Digging deep into the strength and courage she had developed following years of criticism, put downs, bullying and assaults, Annie was tougher and more resourceful than ever.

She would spend hours looking at her options, thinking about what to do. Torn between disappointing the father whom she loved so much, and disappointing herself, Annie, chose to go to her assigned careers advisor.

It was decided she would put in a request for her preference of a career in nursing. This way she would still doing an honourable career, and it was still in the medical field. It didn't have the obvious managerial skills to it, but it was something she could see herself doing, even though she would still be around sick people all day. This would please her dad, give her options, and have more variety in the day to day work. It was a win-win in her mind, and the birthing of her diplomatic nature which would see her experience many wins throughout her life and career.

Although, that said, the diplomacy didn't always extend to other areas of Annie's life.

Challenging the rules and the way things were done was becoming something of the norm for Annie. Wagging school when she didn't want to go to lessons, resisting doing the things she didn't want to do, asking questions such as "Why do we have to do it?" she became braver and more confident each time; especially given that the adults around didn't have an answer for the questions Annie gave them.

Although taking a stand for herself and this rebellious streak never led to problems with the authorities outside of the home, the authority figure at home called 'Mum' was still finding reasons to control Annie.

By contrast, there was always plenty of laughter, hugs and love whenever Annie visited her Russian mama a few suburbs away. Indulging in French and Russian food, often a combination of both, Annie would listen and laugh the hours away. Life with her mama was so different to the neat nastiness experienced at home and she loved the atmosphere.

Mama was eccentric, always having fun and so full of wonderful stories Annie couldn't help but listen to the endless tales which would flow from this incredible woman. Little did Annie know at this time just how inspiring this wonderful lady truly was, she was just simply Mama, the warm and loving grandma who filled Annie's heart with joy.

When not escaping with her mama into one of her stories, Annie would listen to the stories her grandad would tell. Each month without fail, he would gift her a soft drink and bag of chips whilst he would spin yarn after yarn, always exciting, always loving.

Unbeknownst to Annie, she had already mastered the gift of bouncing back and rising higher each time something unpleasant happened. Her ability to find joy in any given moment, to bring warmth and laughter to the lives of others, whilst dealing with her own challenges was something that came naturally to Annie. A total surfer babe and incredibly beautiful in the most natural of ways, Annie turned heads without even noticing. Her laugh would make others smile, her smile was never just on her face, but shone from every part of her. She was stunning in looks, energy and wit; again, something she was unaware of due to the negative self-talk she had adopted.

Was it jealousy her mother felt? Was it her mother's own pain, feelings of rejection and low self-confidence she was projecting on Annie? Whatever it was, the more her mother rejected her, the closer Annie grew to her father.

---

1. HSC – The Australian High School Certificate taken at the age of 17

Seize and treasure magic moments, they are your forever memories

Chapter Six
BECOMING ATTRACTIVE

The next couple of years Annie would throw herself into her studies. Not being hugely academic, but enjoying the learning process, she would need to focus more than some of her friends on remembering the finer details such as dates and names.

Her dad was right, maths wasn't her strongest subject, but that never stopped Annie, she simply learnt how to get around it and do what was needed. Study sessions and days at the beach with her friends were always filled with fun and laughter. No longer haunted by the crushing blows of the past, and no longer thinking about the need to purge, Annie's life was turning around for the better.

She was enjoying sports and being active, enough for her to enjoy without the fear of death or hospitalisation as a result of severe asthma attacks. Being active also gave Annie the energy and self-belief she needed. The more active she was, the more she grew in confidence that she could do more. It also helped keep her body weight in check without the need to starve herself or purge which made her smile from ear to. ear.

With everything Annie had experienced, she had become very switched on about many different aspects of life. Always helpful and respectful, even if cheeky and rebellious with it, Annie was a delight to be around. Vivacious and always full of life, her and her friends would bring the life and soul to each gathering they attended, whether that was with the church, house parties or simply getting together with friends down on the beach.

One of Annie's greatest passions was social work, and with the amount of life experience she had already gained, this was a line of work Annie would be able to make a huge difference in. Learning of the mission work the church did also resonated with Annie on a deep level. Her desire to help others through life was obvious and acknowledged by many in the church community. With the pastoral and social care events held at the church, Annie would volunteer, and the more she got involved, the more inspired she became about creating positive change in the world.

With a love of helping others, her passion for mission and social work combined with her intended career in nursing, the size of Annie's heart was obvious for all to see, well almost all. Her mother still refused to acknowledge it, even though it would have been hard for her to not see the beautiful young woman her daughter was becoming. With the effervescent energy she exuded, it was hard not to be happy in Annie's company; but with the jealousy of Annie her mother harboured deep down inside of her, she was blinded to just how truly blessed she was to be Annie's mother.

At the age 17, her final year of high school, this kindness to others, endless energy and natural beauty wouldn't go unnoticed for much longer by members of the opposite sex.

With the arrival of invitation to join her friend Oliver for his 21st birthday, it was party time for Annie and her friends from church. As always Annie and her group of friends would be chatting and laughing the night away, bringing a level of liveliness and dynamism that would distract a certain young man the whole evening long.

His current relationship had come to an end that very evening, and some would say this was divine timing as this particular young man couldn't help but look over and smile to himself.

Who was this beautiful bleached blonde young woman, with a laugh so infectious it made everyone smile? His attraction to her was instant, and soon they began chatting. At the end of the party they both stayed behind to help clean up. The more they chatted, the more he liked her, and when the opportunity arose at the end of the night to drive her home, he took it.

It was an instant attraction for both of them, and soon enough Annie got to call this surfer dude named James her man. Swapping stories of their travels, including James's recent trip to Thailand and Annie's to Bali, they discovered they had a lot more in common than first thought. Both had a passion for mission work, both were competitive and they both had an insane crush on each other.

The youngest of five children, James saw himself and his family as quite kooky compared to Annie's super cool family. Little did he know about the stuff going on behind this incredible smile, which not only lit up every space the new love of his life was in, but also lit the flames of passion deep within him.

Annie would sit and sunbathe on the beach, reading and watching her man surf the waves, feeling incredibly excited and lucky to have fallen for such a cool guy. Little did she know he too couldn't quite believe his luck that this stunning and exciting young woman wanted to be his sweetheart.

She made him want to be a better man, her protector and within two years, James proposed to his spunky beach babe who had enriched his life in so many ways. The proposal took place in Annie's family home in the front room, with no bells and whistles, shooting stars or a sunset walk on the beach, just a knowing from James that it was going to happen right there in that moment.

Now with both of them being part of the church community, and being pretty switched on individuals, they both agreed to attend the pastoral care programmes designed with young loves in mind. With pre-marriage guidance and counselling delivered by members of the church community, Annie and James were ready to take on anything together; and they would need to be for the challenges that lay ahead.

As with everything to do with Annie, her mother was not happy, and sadly this time, neither was her dad. They did not approve of teenage marriages and they would make it known that such marriages would end in divorce. With her mum telling James not to marry her 'because she's got issues' the pre-marriage counselling sessions came in very handy.

But nothing would deter these two lovebirds from tying the knot, James had lit that Sagittarian fire within Annie, and it was never going out.

Sunbathing topless on the beach was common back in the mid-eighties, before the skin cancer scares engulfed the world, and it was something Annie had grown in body confidence to do. With the summer sun increasing temperatures all around, and with Annie reading on the beach, taking sneak peeks at her hunk in the water, soaking up all the vitamin D she could, it was not unheard of for her to send temperatures soaring with her beautiful figure. A few of James's friends noticed, and yet in true Annie style she didn't notice the wide-open mouths of these grown men at a loss for words; just one of the many things James loved about her.

As plans for the wedding started, both Annie and James agreed it made sense to have a summer wedding, and so in December 1987 – just one week after Annie had turned 20, a sign of her respectful rebellion – the two love struck sweethearts were married.

As with every bride, looking her best was important to Annie. Although already beautiful, it was time to get in better shape and allow her freshly dyed blonde hair to grow long. Her mum had always kept her hair short because apparently she would never be able to take care of it long, but Annie was determined to show her mother, and herself, that she was a lot more capable than the limits which had been imposed upon her in previous years.

With James in his light grey suit and matching bow tie, the jacket cropped at the waist with a cummerbund, as was the height of fashion in those days, and Annie with her blonde curls up pinned up and fixed in place with a tiara of baby's-breath, showing off her neckline and shoulders in her sweetheart off the shoulder lace bodice dress with full skirting, those in attendance knew this was a match made in heaven.

James was still in the process of studying at Bible college and with married quarters on campus, it made sense for the young couple to set up their first home together on campus. Annie was studying to become a nurse at university and doing her practical work at the Royal North Shore hospital, which was only a 50-minute train ride from Burwood. Everything was working out beautifully. Husband and wife were both working, making plans for their future and life was getting even more exciting. This new life brought new opportunities and new friends, and with new friends came new adventures and memories. James was enjoying his time with his soccer friends at weekly matches, and Annie enjoyed the company of her new friends at the university and the hospital.

Nightly trips to the gym also brought with it a newfound confidence for Annie as well as helping her sculpt a 'gym body'. Many others thought of her as sporty, but other than the nights at the gym, intermittent cycling and walking, Annie was anything but sporty.

After searching for a home away from campus, James and Annie found a tiny one-bedroom apartment in Manly. Although slightly on the damp side, it was near the beach, close to where James worked as an optician, and a bus ride to Royal North Shore hospital for Annie. Creating a life and home together was magical and although they were not in one of the best units, it didn't matter; it was home, and it was filled with love, laughter and lively non-stop conversations.

An open house for friends and family alike, the apartment soon became a warm and welcoming home, and with their careers and family goals in place, the young couple flourished.

With so many life changes going on, a holiday was needed so with plans made for a three-month trip to Thailand there was something else to look forward to. It was time for the couple to kick back and relax, allowing all the external transformations to really settle. Reflecting on her life, and offering gratitude up to God, thanking Him for all her blessings, Annie couldn't be happier.

A lot had happened in her short life and here she was with James, her beloved, in Thailand with friends enjoying life to the full. The way she felt about herself as a woman, as a person, was lighter, more positive and little did she know she was about to embark upon a whole new version of herself.

With this new transformation about to take place, James, or rather Jamie as he was known back in those days, would be thrown into the middle of a gauntlet that would see him stand up against his new mother-in-law and honour his wife in a way that would cause a path of egg shells to be laid for ever more.

Stay clear of drama, it loves to suck your energy and time

Chapter Seven

DEAR ANNIE

Although I am supposed to become a pharmacist, I'm currently becoming a nurse even though I actually want to become a businesswoman. This is going to sound weird but sometimes I secretly wish I was a man so I could have enrolled in an MBA straight out of school.

Crazy right!?

Is my adult life as a woman really going to be this complicated? My ovaries seem to have dominated the tone of expectation on me to date and I'm not feeling a strong desire to deactivate my 'Boss Girl' tendencies without a good hard fight.

Why can't I just be me?

Doesn't every young woman just want to be the person they were born to be? Sometimes I feel like I'm going to burst with the pure volume of ambitious possibilities that I try to imagine as a future reality. Like my dream of working for the United Nations running aid projects in Africa or building fair trade businesses which support women and children living in poverty and bondage.

I must admit, I'm not feeling confident my dreams are even possible, but my beautiful grandmothers have shown me that women with purpose, passion and need can rise above their station so I better start believing that magic can happen. I like to think I model myself on their pioneering spirit, tenacity and bravery.

To be honest I am feeling the magic already. Since meeting and falling in love with James, I feel safe, secure and happy. I love the fun and adventure we experience exploring nature together and dig that he enjoys my curious mind and quirky nature.

Apparently, I'm refreshing, and my never-ending chatter doesn't bother him – Amazing! He does however get annoyed when I get defensive and feisty about stupid rules made by annoying people who limit my freedom. So, I'm currently trying my hardest to tone myself down and be a more palatable person, so I don't get hurt, rejected or left alone. That is my nightmare.

Our only fights seem to be when I feel he doesn't support me during clashes with my mum and boy does that make me go nuts. Apparently, his role is to keep the peace and siding with her does this. I definitely need help to unpack some lifelong trauma here.

I hope I can be inspirational like my grandmothers and ideally, I'd love to do it in feminine heels with grace and style.

I wish I had a plan, but it seems like I'll have to do life my way.

Hopefully, my fellow women will become more collaborative and less competitive along this journey as there is so much more joy in healing each other.

I'm sure my journey will involve breaking and rewriting some rules along the way but hey, that sounds like fun to me.

I'm going to do what it takes to become Annie and learn to love the skin I'm in.

Keep believing in me,

love Anne-Marie xo

Strive for synergy, the impact is explosive

Chapter Eight
BECOMING ANNIE

Enjoying the company of friends and the heat of the Thai nights, Anne-Marie would soon become a name of the past. So much had changed in Annie's life and with the newfound freedom of being married and living in her own home with the man she adored, it was inevitable a new identity was on its way.

Being referred to as 'Jamie and Annie', put a smile on Annie's face at the same time she exclaimed, "Ooo I like that!" Although not an intentional name change, simply an introduction which had a smoother flow to it making it easier for the couple's Thai friends to pronounce, it would prove to be a complete game changer for Annie. Considering this new nickname, how it felt lighter, fresher, happier, the internal resonance was one of complete synergy and reflected with where Annie was now at in her life.

Speaking with James, she chose to keep this new name, and friends adapted really quickly. The transition was as light as the name itself and so out went the old clunky name of Anne-Marie making way for the arrival of Annie, a woman who was a rule unto herself and destined to change the world.

Telling her mother wasn't quite as easy though and brought the wrath of the wrong kind of Mama Fire to the fore. Annie's mum hated this new name and took it as a blow of rejection as her name Marie had been removed, whereas her dad liked the positive change it brought about in his daughter and this was all that mattered. Once again Annie received the love and support from her dad whilst more bricks were built in the wall between the two feisty Montgomery women.

With young Jamie wanting to keep the peace between mother and daughter, and be respectful to both his wife and mother-in-law, he would face looks of fierce frowning action from Annie if he called her Anne-Marie in front of her mother, and scowls dangerous enough to drive the fiercest of warriors running if he called Annie by her new name in front of her mother.

As with all great (and sensible) husbands, he chose to honour his wife's choice of name and allow his mother-in-law to deal with her own emotions and angst, knowing it had nothing to do with Annie rejecting her mother and everything to do with embracing the woman she was born to be; and boy was she about to embrace it!

You only achieve what you truly believe

Chapter Nine
BECOMING NURSE ANNIE

Knowing she would never have a career in the family business, Annie pursued the career of nursing as discussed with her career's advisor years earlier; and although her choice of career didn't involve working side by side with her dad every day, he was pleased with her choice of career.

Annie was enjoying the balance of studying and working, balancing the theory with the practical, learning and implementing straight away was the best way for her to excel in everything she was doing and becoming.

Studying at the University of Technology, Annie was flourishing, making space in their busy work and study schedules for the things they loved meant Annie could still enjoy lying on the beach reading and sunbathing whilst stealing glances at her handsome hubby as he surfed the waves. Cycling and walking in nature also meant they got a break from the suburbs and provided them with a balanced lifestyle, a lifestyle which also meant Annie was able to keep the weight off; not that James cared about her weight, but it was still something that crept up into the fore of her mind every now and then.

The days of anorexia nervosa and bulimia may be over, but like everyone who has ever been through either of these eating disorders, it is something that stayed with Annie for years to come. Would they raise their ugly heads again when she became pregnant? And what if she had a daughter? Would the daughter have weight issues, and if she did, how would Annie deal with it? Would her own insecurities send her into a tailspin and see her become the overbearing mother or would she be the most incredible, supportive mother any daughter could wish for?

Having been through so much, Annie was able to excel in her nursing due to the understanding she had gained about herself, she may not have known all the academic side of things to begin with, but she knew what it was like to not be listened to, and to go through trauma. She also knew what it was like to have to work things out by herself and didn't want others to have to go through things alone.

Applying her own experiences with the training, and the science, it didn't take Annie long to master the talent of bed side manners and the empathy needed when dealing with patients and their families. In fact, Nurse Annie didn't just remain in the hospital or the classroom, Nurse Annie ran through every fibre of her body. Always caring for others, always there to listen, something lost in a lot of nurses and medical professionals today due to the long and exhausting working hours.

Between work and study, Annie and James continued to attend the coaching and mentoring sessions hosted by their church, believing "if you've got something good make it better". Not only was it useful, it was insightful and enjoyable. Both were loved and deeply embedded within their church community, and they would be called upon to mentor those thinking about getting married. Being served and being of service went hand in hand for both of them, and on any one day they would be helping to host events for up to twenty couples from a variety of different backgrounds in attendance.

In 1989 Annie qualified as a Registered Nurse and had by now developed a love of learning like never before. Her curiosity about the different aspects of nursing, the different ailments, illnesses and diseases were just fascinating for Annie, as well as the different ways to identify the cause and treat the effect of each patient's health problems.

With more money coming in and with the two-year anniversary of being in the one-bed apartment in Manly, it was time to start home hunting again. Something bigger this time, and it wasn't long before a four-bedroom property in Allambie Heights became theirs. A suburb which was developed in the late 1940s and named using the Aboriginal word "Allambie" meaning "peaceful place". A place steeped in historical references from the second world war, and home to the Manly Dam which runs through the South West corner of the area.

Not too far from the Northern beaches, and with the Garigal National Park on its Western Border, Allambie Heights is home to many Aboriginal Rock Carvings in the Gambooya Reserve. A place of beauty and the perfect start to the new chapter in their lives.

With all the extra rooms in their new home, Annie and James filled them with possibilities. Children were always part of the future plans for the happy couple, but it wasn't quite time for children yet.

Being friendly, welcoming open-hearted people, Annie and James would host homestay guests from around the world. With both men and women from countries such as Germany, Korea, Japan, Switzerland and Brazil staying for a few weeks, sometimes even months, there was never a shortage of conversation and cultural exchange going on. Many would come to learn English, and both hosts and guests were only too happy to have a conversation, not to mention a party or two. With up to twenty or thirty people at any one time in attendance at a barbeque you can guarantee laughter filled the air and there were more than one or two dry mouths the mornings following the shenanigans the night before!

With some of the homestay guests being in their late twenties and early thirties, and in the process of a career change, there was always an opportunity for both hosts and guests to share their stories, experiences in the work place and be inspired by each other. Cultural exchanges on family dynamics, belief systems, travel and adventures, as well as social structures, conversation never ran dry.

With a couple of years gone by, Annie was now working full time in the hospital and seeing what was possible with her career growth. She knew deep down she wanted a family, that had never been in question, but Annie was loving her work. Taking care of people, meeting new faces every day, new and exciting things happening all the time, although not quite as exciting for the patients, Annie enjoyed her work immensely. With the ability to stay calm and positive even in the scariest of situations and the most stressful moments, Annie was an asset to both the medical teams and the patients. Nurse Annie, a modern-day Florence Nightingale, was glad she had chosen to become a nurse, rather than pleasing her father by going to work in the pharmacy.

Thoughts were coming to the fore of her mind about what was possible for her as she watched the Dr's and Senior members of the hospital staff. With ideas and drive, she knew one day some of these ideas would eventually come to fruition, but Annie wouldn't have the time to think about those ideas just yet, especially not with the events which were about to unfold and change her life forever.

Time is precious, use it wisely

Chapter Ten

BECOMING PARENTS

With the plan to have a large family, three to four children would be ideal, the couple started trying for a baby. Unfortunately, the first pregnancy resulted in a miscarriage, a difficult time for the young lovers but with the support from each other they shed tears and bounced back.

In 1990 just three-and-a-half years after Annie and James tied the knot, they received the wonderful news that they were in fact pregnant with their first child. Thankfully, Annie's fertility hadn't been affected by the anorexia nervosa in her early teens, as it does with many women, especially if those who have not started their periods by the age of fifteen.

With the additional income from the homestays on top of their salaries, both Annie and James would have enough money to nurse and feed the new baby. Even though the ongoing mentoring at church, and the firm belief that God always provides, there were still numerous questions and doubts being raised in the young couple's minds These questions were pretty normal questions and doubts of any mother and father, regardless of age, income and support system would have. Annie's dad had always said that taking care of a baby meant she wouldn't be able to work long hours running a business, and nursing was long hours; would she have to give up her work?

They would both soon realise through the support of family and the church these questions were pretty normal questions and doubts of any mother and father, regardless of age, income and support system would have. Annie's dad had always said that taking care of a baby meant she wouldn't be able to work long hours running a business, and nursing was long hours; would she have to give up her work?

As with all new parents there was a lot of thinking to do, a lot of planning and a lot of sleepless nights, and not just after the baby was born.

Staying with them at the time was one of their Homestay guests called Benedict from Switzerland. He was more a member of the family than a homestay guest, and he was delighted to share in the celebrations of this wonderful news.

Leading up to the day of the first ultrasound scan, and with twins on both sides of the family, jokes were made about the possibility of twins, but the thought of having twins didn't really register, and nor does it for most parents until they see and hear their new addition on the ultrasound screen and beat of the tiny heart. As Annie and James had no benchmark to relate the size of Annie's bump to a previous pregnancy the jokes were simply passed off as jokes, and they would simply wait and see what they would be blessed with.

James had taken some time off work to join Annie for their first important event as parents. As they both held hands and looked at each other, and then at the ultrasound screen in the hospital, excitement and anticipation building, Annie let out a nervous giggle as the cold gel was applied to her belly. With the doctor moving the wand of the ultrasound scanner firmly across Annie's tummy, a smile broke out because the sight and sound of not one, but two babies were seen and heard. Mouths and eyes wide open, giggles and smiles aplenty, and the confirmation of twins delighted the soon to be parents. Twins! Two babies for the price of one, talk about being efficient Annie and James!

Striding excitedly out of the hospital on his way back to work, having said goodbye to his beloved, James and Benedict caught sight of each other from across Manly Corso. Hands cupped around his mouth Benedict calls out to James, "Is it twins?"

James, laughing and full of joy, cupped his hands around his mouth shouts back in celebration, "It's twins!" Both men overjoyed with the news, waving a celebratory and joyful fist in the air at each other continued on their way, with Benedict stopping on his way home to collect not just one, but two bottles of champagne... well a bottle for each baby made sense! They would have had a bottle for each if they were single babies, so why not two for twins?

As the news spread to family and friends, and was shared at work, everything seemed to be going beautifully. However, one friend wasn't so happy and given the situation it was understandable. Annie had been friends with this woman for many years. They had spent hours upon hours over the years planning their weddings, their families and imaging all that would happen for them both.

However, this particular friend had experienced multiple heart-breaking miscarriages; something neither of them had anticipated whilst planning the perfect futures. Annie being a devoted friend, had supported her friend through this painful time, held her friend whilst she cried, cheered her up and helped her through the darkest days. Hearing of Annie's happy news, especially being pregnant with twins was just too much for her friend to bear. The pain her friend felt, the jealousy and resentment, the sense of her own loss was creating a distance between the two friends, and eventually resulted in the friendship never being able to recover.

The sadness Annie felt for her friend, and the loss of the friendship was difficult, but the joy of becoming a mother and sharing this beautiful journey into parenthood with the most gorgeous guy there ever was, was too much to dampen her joy and excitement.

Adjusting to motherhood is challenging enough for any woman especially seeing your belly and breasts swell to incredible sizes. As this was her first pregnancy, Annie had nothing to compare the pregnancy of twins to, so in true Annie style it was simply business as usual. Going to work, going to the gym and giggling with her handsome husband, Annie was incredibly happy. Whilst her dad was overjoyed at the thought of becoming a grandpa of twins, her mother worried aloud, "How are you going to cope?"

It didn't seem as though anything Annie did, or didn't do, would be enough, so again Annie being Annie chose to focus on the positives and put a smile on her face. During a time when a woman really needs her mother, Annie was still trying to figure out the dynamic and keep the peace, but it wasn't stopping her being excited about the journey she and James were embarking upon.

As the pregnancy continued into the second and third trimester, Annie couldn't stop itching. "It feels like shards of glass are cutting through my skin," she would say to James, and although there was no rash, and nothing to be seen, the itching sensation became a worry. Was it the washing powder? Mosquito bites? The dreaded sand-flies? Nope, nothing had changed.

After a short while and process of elimination, it was time for a visit to the doctors. A quick examination and consultation and Annie's told she had cholestasis; a severe itching caused by the slow flow of bile from the liver, believed to be caused by the body being unable to break down the fats within the body. Although there is no clear and confirmed cause of the ailment, it is known to occur in many pregnant women in the third trimester of pregnancy, especially expectant mums of multiple births. Normally restricted to the hands and feet, with incessant itching made worse at night, cholestasis isn't normally dangerous.

Annie being Annie, and not one to do things by halves, was dealt the full body blow of the itching all over her body; just what she needed with her ever expanding twin tummy and blossoming boobs! The only concerns to consider were the potential risk of preterm babies and lung problems due to the inhaling of the meconium, and in very rare cases a stillborn child.

Luckily though both babies were as efficient as their mother and chose to bring things along at their own pace. With just four to five weeks left to go, two healthy boys wriggled their way out into the world. One of them however was slightly more relaxed about his arrival and chose to come out in style laying transverse and 40 minutes after his slightly older brother named Caleb. Although some would say this was fashionably late, it was somewhat worrying and talk of having a C-section was in the air. Wanting to live life on his own terms, Daniel the younger of the twins, chose to come out when he was ready, and not a moment before. This was his entrance into the world, and he was going to do it his way.

With the birth of two beautiful twin boys, life was busy and the nursing of others in the hospital became nursing of a different kind at home. Absolutely nailing the pre pregnancy shape almost straight away, a dream for most mothers, Annie adjusted well to twin motherhood. Well, what other choice was there? Getting into the rhythm of life with Daniel and Caleb, with both parents back to work, Annie part time, Annie's heart skipped a beat again.

Was she indeed pregnant again? You bet she was, but sadly this baby was not to make it into the world and was miscarried like the first baby. Digging deep into James' love, throwing herself into parenting the boys, and working part time at the hospital, life continued as was now the new normal. Shortly after Annie's heartbeat skipped again and this time baby number three was getting comfortable for the bumpy ride ahead.

Now the thought of becoming pregnant again less than two years after a set of twins graces the family may sound like a crazy idea, in fact according to Annie's mum she was crazy, and not just in the joking sense of the word either. She hadn't been happy the first time around and now Annie was pregnant again, she couldn't stop herself from telling Annie it would cost two hundred and twenty thousand dollars a year to raise just one child, so how on earth did James and Annie think they could afford to raise yet another child when they already had two?

As the days rolled by, the jokes about another set of twins being on the way were coming thick and fast. With three sets of twins in Annie's grandmother's cousin's family and James' sister having a set of twins, it wasn't as if twins were unexpected, but the thought of two sets of twins just wasn't on the cards of expectation. That was until the date of the ultrasound scan drew closer. Thoughts swirling around in James' mind, the friendly teasing from friends and colleagues, all of it had been like water off a duck's back.

The words, "You're quite big for your time of pregnancy," delivered by the midwife peaked James' attention. What if it was a second set of twins? They already had one set, and although their home was big enough, and they still had everything from the birth of Daniel and Caleb, it was their own human capacity James was concerned about. The stresses on Annie's body, four children under three years old, work, homestays, and the devastating news that Annie's dad now had a brain tumour and only had six to 12 months to live, were all swimming through James' mind and crashing over him like the waves he surfed. Life in that moment was unfolding in slow motion. Each and every look from the doctor, to Annie's belly, to the screen to his beautiful wife's face, back to the screen and then the news he had been dreading, but somewhere deep inside of him was the simmering joy of a dad to be, he was going to be a dad again, to two more babies.

Shock gripped his body, could this be happening? Twins again? He looked at Annie who was smiling through her own shock, back to the screen, back at Annie, legs slightly weaker than the moments before, and the cascade of emotions raining over him. This was going to take some processing, and as the numbness of shock transported him back to work as a retail optical dispenser, and as he graced the shop floor, some of his colleagues knew from the look on his face it was twins, others called out "Well Gibbo, is it twins?" to which he just looked at them and nodded. Twins. Again. Four children. Job done. No more. Quicker than expected, and most definitely in the most unexpected of ways, but they had got the children they wanted, now it was time to buckle up and enjoy the ride.

Once they were over the initial shock, the lovestruck couple laughed at their own efficiency and the unexpected turn of events; but when Annie's mother found out, yet another tirade came Annie's way in the accusation that she was overpopulating the world and would not be able to manage.

Most mothers would be excited at the opportunity to get involved, and some would thrive in taking over the situation, but not Annie's mum. Her dad on the other hand, battling painful muscle seizures, was concerned about how the young couple would manage with four children all under 26 months of age. That said he was delighted to be told he would be a grandpa again, something to take his mind off his own health and give him joy. Benedict, their homestay guest and now dear friend was now back in Switzerland and was delighted with the news… and another two bottles of champagne was purchased and drunk in celebration.

Annie continued with a couple of night duties for 4 months throughout the pregnancy, but soon had to give those up as the due date drew nearer. She could tell the babies were going to be early again, and this time the babies were going to need more rest, and so was she. As the weeks passed by, Annie's belly was swelling quickly, and at 28 weeks the feeling of glass shards under the skin were back. Showers, scratching, sleepless nights and a steely determination, Annie took it all in her stride; well what else was there to do? It's not as if there was a miracle cure, so the only way to deal with it was suck it up and get on with it.

With the itching of the cholestasis burning under her skin, and the unborn twins needing to get out of their mum's tum sooner than expected, Annie was admitted to Manly Hospital for the birth, this time a C-section would be needed as both babies were lying breech. Several hours later, the Gibbins family was blessed with the arrival of baby Samuel and to start evening out the hormones further down the years, baby Hannah who arrived shortly after, although not as fashionably late as her older brother Daniel chose to be.

With three boys and one girl to look after, both Annie and James were feeling the strain of what seemed like endless sleepless nights, nappy changes, feeding and dressing. Not to worry though, with friends cooking meals and rallying around them all, life was still a bundle of fun. Homestay guests were not as frequent but when they did arrive, they certainly got more than they bargained for. Annie returned to work for a couple of nightshifts a week for some much needed money and to keep her mind active and away from the dark cloud of her dad's health, which if she had allowed it to, could have engulfed her.

Being Dad to two sets of twins wasn't as insane as James had expected, and settled into the joys of having three sons and a daughter, a daughter who would come to adore her father and take great pleasure in being 'Daddy's little girl' whenever she could. With Daniel and Caleb now toddling around the home and starting to chatter away, there was never any shortness of amusement and joy in the Allamabie Heights home, even if it was no longer a place of peace in the silent aspect of the word.

Annie's dad was still powering on through and showing no real inclination of leaving this world, especially with 4 young grandchildren to care for and play with. They had given him hope and a renewed sense of energy, something he needed. It didn't stop Annie considering the inevitable though. With the state of her dad's health always lurking in the shadows at the back of her mind, Annie chose to simply get on with life and not dwell on the thought of 'when would *the* call come? Would she be with the kids, at work or in the middle of a nappy change?' It wouldn't matter when the call came, all that mattered whilst he was alive, and until such time that the call came, it was business as usual. She had to be strong throughout all this, for herself, her children and for her dad. He was her rock, the man who challenged her in so many ways and he made her even more determined than ever to prove him wrong about the modern-day working mother. She was going to show her dad just what she was made of, and make him the proudest, happiest dad there was.

But first she had to address the gypsy soul and curiosity within her which was starting to stir again. With four young children all under three, moving home was just not on the cards, but then with Annie and James life was full of surprises and that wasn't about to change any time soon.

When Mummy's not happy, nobody is happy

Chapter Eleven

BECOMING EXHAUSTED

Toddlers, two pre-schoolers and work, there was not much time to take a rest, and as with most mums with young children, everything was about making sure the family had everything they needed. With everything that had happened in her life so far, Annie had learnt to be resilient and strong by herself. James has changed all that and even though they had been married for a decade there were still times when just getting on with everything by herself was the best way to move forward.

Family gatherings provided high levels of stress for Annie as she worried about the safety of her children when in the presence of their uncle. The Mama Fire burned within Annie and it was fuelling what was eventually going to become a raging fire; but for now it was simmering, a constant simmer put aside so life could continue in the most positive of ways, but with tiredness increasing, it wouldn't be long before something had to give.

Annie's health had been impacted following the birth of Daniel and Caleb when post-pregnancy asthma had flared up, causing several serious asthma attacks; inviting smugness from her mother and the looks of 'I told you so'.

When the asthma attacks returned again following the birth of Samuel and Hannah, tiredness rose to a whole new level especially with the large quantities of milk Annie's body was producing. The amount of milk being expressed didn't go unnoticed and soon gained Annie the nickname 'Daisy'. With enough milk to go round for all the family to have a 'cuppa tea' with if needed, and still have enough to be thrown away, Annie's body was working overtime. James feeding the babies had helped but there was still a lot of catching up on sleep to do, especially as sleepless nights were regular due to also working night shifts at the hospital.

As with most mums there was just no time for Annie to just simply be, for her body to recuperate and recharge itself; or so we all lead ourselves to be true at the time.

As Daniel and Caleb were approaching five years of age, with Hannah and Samuel approaching three years old, the Gibbins home was always lively and busy. Playdates, tiny tears tantrums, birthday parties and as most parents with under-fives soon discover, the children had busier social lives than they did!

Annie was still getting itchy feet, but this time it had nothing to do with the cholestasis, and everything to do with her gypsy soul wanting to move on again. James being a settled and happy to stay put persona, was in no hurry to move, but if his beautiful wife wanted to move, then he would give her what she wanted. She was the love of his life, and as they say, 'Happy wife, happy life', and he wanted his wife to be happy always.

With the laws of attraction working as they do; all we have to do is focus on the outcome, create a high vibe energetic state of being and take aligned action to manifest our dreams. Some of us are better at it than others, and sometimes manifesting what we want takes us on a journey and we are provided with experiences we could never dream of. With Annie always being focused and in a high vibe state pretty much all of the time, regardless of what is going on in the world, manifesting the next home move would come sooner than she thought, and this time smelling of roses would take on a whole new meaning, at least to begin with.

With the kids in bed, and an early night planned, the weather outside was dull and gloomy. With the air pressure heavy, James and Annie knew there was a storm on the way, but nothing could have prepared them for what the next 24 hours would bring. The wind was strong and singing a wild song, howling in pain and unleashing it's fury, with a downpour of nonstop rain to match the temper tantrums of the fiercest two year old or the heartbreak of a lost love, but not even that was enough to wake the pair from their much needed sleep. The wakeup call came for James at

6am when Daniel wanted to know why the floors were all wet. Thinking a sink was overflowing or the toilet had been locked, James woke himself up ready to tackle the taps and stopcock; but oh no, Annie had manifested something much bigger for them to deal with in her desire to move home.

With feet now in several centimetres of water throughout the single-story home, James was fully awake and yelling at Annie to wake her up from her much-needed sleep. The house, which was situated on a large concrete slab foundation was flooded, and the water was rising… and it wasn't the aroma of coffee that was waking them up with each inhale either! Springing into action, and into the rising water, it soon came apparent due to the foul stench where the water was coming from.

With the deep natural instinct of parental protection of the young rising deep within both James and Annie, a phone call was the first thing on the agenda. With a faster than normal speed of explanation and organisation, Annie and James were soon handing all four children over the garden fence, in their pyjamas, to the neighbours for breakfast and an early morning playdate. Next on the agenda was figuring out what was actually going on, and where the water was coming into the property. It wasn't the kitchen, but it was the bathrooms and the laundry room, and everything on the floor throughout the home had to be destroyed due to sewerage contamination. Another phone call later and the plumbers and emergency teams were on their way; and so were the emotions and tears, but there was no time for that, so the emotions and tears got pushed down, the courage pulled to the surface and the game faces applied.

In no time at all the source of the problem was identified as the pine tree penetration into the sewerage pipes, with the build-up of refuse in the pipes looking for a way out. The storm had brought with it a vast amount of water and the only way for the piping to cope with the pressure was to send it up and out into the Gibbins' home.

Seeing the plumbers and emergency teams take over, it was now time for the build-up of pressure to be released from Annie. Finding a place to sit down, she let out the build-up of emotions, those from the morning, and those which had been building up within her like silent assassins. She was exhausted and this event had brought it all to the surface.

With nature providing a mirror to the constant drain on her own energy and resources over the last couple of decades, Annie sobbed her heart out. As she watched her home being emptied one toy, one shoe and one piece of furniture at a time, her heart broke. Everything her and James had been building together, being tossed out, contaminated by the urine and faeces of other people's lives, and now they were going to have to put on another pair of brave faces for the children. Walking around to the neighbours and explaining what had happened, things were being arranged for the family of six to stay in a hotel until things were arranged for something more permanent. The children were excited and ready for this 'great adventure' and life in a hotel, but James and Annie were shattered. Completely exhausted and in need of a break.

As the days and the weeks rolled into months, and with one rental property after another falling short, landlords not delivering and a flea invested place which needed a quick exit, the stress was proving too much. Without the security of a place to call home, things were challenging to say the least, and it is moments like this that the marriage counselling came into its own. Whilst the house clean-up took place, and option after option was explored, it was decided they would sell the home and buy a plot of land so they could build their own home; because what else do you do with four children under four at the age of twenty-seven, and a home damaged by sewerage?

The level of exhaustion was really beginning to take its toll and friends were noticing how tired Annie was looking, as was James, so it was no surprise to him when their closest friends took him to one side and told him, "Annie needs a break, you both do, away from the children, just the two of you."

James agreed, and thought it was a great idea, so with the help and support of their friends he arranged for each child to stay with their friends, at four different family homes. A break from each other would do them all good, and although Annie took some convincing about how on earth the children would survive a moment without them both, and how they could afford this when they needed every cent they had to put towards building their family home, she soon relented when one of her dear friends told her she needed to take a break and stop to take care of herself. Annie's tiredness had increased dramatically, and anything and everything was creating a constant flow of tears.

James was in full-on superhero mode and had arranged everything: the individual holidays for all the children, and booked him and his beautiful wife into a tropical island getaway for the weekend. As he held her in his arms, looked into her eyes he said the words that all tired mums wish to hear, "When Mummy's not happy, nobody's happy. Let's get you smiling again," and then he sealed those two sentences with a passionate kiss, with Annie relenting and allowing herself to be whisked away for a well overdue, and well deserved break with the man she loved with all her heart.

Emotion overload, missing the children, and wanting to settle her mind, Annie called the children the first night they were away. Between the excitement of each call with each child telling her they were having a great time, a quick 'I miss you' and 'I love you, bye!' Annie allowed herself to relax, smile and unwind. With palm trees, walks on the beach, cocktails and the biggest prize of all, an uninterrupted lie in, Annie allowed herself to be loved on by James, and recharge herself. Mummy guilt was there, but so was the realisation of just how exhausted she was.

Lying by the pool sipping cocktails, Annie relaxed into the sunshine even more. Looking over at the hunk lying beside her, she realised just how much things had gotten way out of hand. The quality time they were having together just being a couple, laughing and playing, they both knew this was no longer a luxury or something frivolous to be put way down the priority list. They were a priority and date nights and quality time together as a couple was a necessity.

Annie had neglected her own wellbeing and sense of self for the sake of others, as do the majority of wives and mothers the world over, but this would have to stop.

How could she be of service to others, if she didn't take care of herself first and foremost?

How could she be the happiest version of self if she was self-sacrificing, not honouring her full potential as a woman in all areas of life?

How could she encourage her children to study and be the best version of themselves if she wasn't doing, and being it herself?

With so many powerful questions flooding her mind in these

moments of relaxation, it was now time to start answering them and find out what was truly possible.

Being still, relaxing and quietening the mind was the gift Annie needed, and James had delivered.

Now with her mind still, it was starting to get curious.

Dream big scary audacious goals and then focus on smashing them

Chapter Twelve
BECOMING MANAGERIAL

With two twin births under her belt, and in the process of selling one home whilst building another, Annie was showcasing the very best in project management skills which she had yet to recognise; but then again being a mother is one of the biggest project management jobs on the market.

James was working full-time, working with Annie in the evenings on the home situation, and being a hands-on father. Teamwork was most definitely making the dream work, and the dream would most definitely need to be worked because life was about to take on another interesting turn of events.

With the family now complete in record speed, it was decided that James would do the honours and put a stop to his sacred seed producing more children. After a visit to family planning, he returned with a vasectomy referral and promptly put it in his bedside cupboard until he could get around to it. Annie dreamed of having one more girl but the thought she could have triplet boys made her stay on the pill. With Daniel and Caleb at school and Hannah and Samuel at pre-school, Annie was flat out juggling four active kids, a husband at work, and daydreaming about if she would ever return to work and if so how. For now, it was time for her to be Nurse Annie, and more importantly time for her to be Annie.

She soon became Nurse Annie at home with four young children picking up coughs and colds, knee scraps and bumps from the rigorous play the four young children enjoyed together. With sickness bugs going around it was no surprise when Caleb started to feel ill, and when it called for a trip to the doctor's Annie went with him, especially as she was feeling sick herself. With Caleb checked over, it was now Annie's turn to be checked over, except this time, it wasn't a sickness bug, baby number five was on the way.

Annie's head was spinning to coincide with the nausea, and it was all just too much to take in. She was extremely stunned to be pregnant while on the pill but also hoping that it was the baby girl she still dreamed of having. When she got home and told James 'the news' the couple stared at each other in disbelief. How were they going to cope with a house build, being in temporary accommodation, selling their other home AND two sets of twins? Oh, and not forgetting work, the time for each of them to excel outside of their marriage as well as in it. Well they just would. It was time to 'suck it up and run with it' whatever 'it' was.

One night Annie had a dream that she was having ten babies and when she delivered them all and wrapped them all up snuggly in a row, James told her she could only keep three. She woke up in a flood of tears telling James I don't want to give away any of my babies!!! "What if it's twins again? And what if, knowing our track record, we end up having triplets!? What then?" The thought of triplets hadn't crossed James' mind, but twins had; and so had the thought of having another little girl. Twin girls would be good, they would be happy with twin girls. One would be better, but not triplets. "Please God don't let it be triplets!" giggled a nervous Annie. One girl please, pretty please.

Always a couple to see the positives from the negatives, Annie and James forged ahead with all of their plans. Why would they not? These were the choices they were making for the future, and although things were hectic and somewhat scary at times, they had each other and they would get through it together. Game faces on, the house build gained more momentum and the other house was sold. Five house moves within a year is more than enough for any young couple, but a young couple with two sets of twins, another one on the way, and a house build, many marriages would have crumbled: but not James and Annie. It was making them stronger and preparing them for the events further down the line.

With two sets of twins, heading into the Ultrasound room at Northshore Hospital, silent prayers were being whispered by both parents. "Please let it be one, and a girl". Gel applied, wand in hand the doctor started scanning Annie's abdomen. James was the more nervous of the two and was so relieved to find out there was only one baby this time; although he did encourage the doctor to keep looking 'just in case one was hiding'. With the confirmation that there was indeed only one child this time, a deep breath he didn't know he was holding escaped and his shoulders released. Annie smiling in relief, and now amusement at the thoughts which had previously gone through their minds, was curious as to how different this pregnancy would be. She'd only experienced twin pregnancies and births before, so to only have to carry and then deliver one baby was a whole new experience.

Breaking the news to her parents brought with it moments of trepidation, but it had to be done, so an invitation to come over to their new home for the afternoon was sent. Having broken the news, Annie's dad was stunned with the news that he was going to become a grandfather again, and a bit concerned with how his daughter and son-in-law would cope. He was also relieved to hear the news there was only one baby on the horizon.

Annie's mother was not so thrilled, in fact she was disgusted and told Annie to "get an abortion, you make me sick!" Confronted by the depth of this nastiness, and the shock felt deep within, Annie's mother wasn't the only one feeling sick. The pain was too much this time and Annie told her mother to leave. How could a mother say such a thing to her own daughter? What must she be going through on the inside to speak such harsh words?

A few days later Annie's dad called and said that her mother was deeply upset about being asked to leave and asked Annie to apologise for throwing her own mother out of the house. A repeating pattern was emerging, Annie's mother would communicate cruel words, Annie would stand up for herself and then her mother would cry and then Annie's dad and James would play peacemakers, resulting in Annie always having to apologise; which she would just to keep the peace. The last thing her dad needed was his wife berating him over their daughter.

Moving into their new home had finally given the family space of their own, to make their own, and no one was going to make it an unpleasant place to be. The large dormer windows allowed the sunlight to fill each room, and with beautiful, almost panoramic views over Allambie Heights, the family settled in. With an intercom system installed throughout the home, it was easy to communicate over the three floors, especially when the children were feeling mischievous and a tad lazy.

The day finally arrived for baby number five to arrive at Manly Hospital, and this time James would be called upon to be more than the father in the waiting room. When the time came to deliver the doctor was nowhere to be found, so rolling up his sleeves it was time for James to step up and be ready to help the midwife when requested. With baby in a good position and Annie comfortable, a natural birth was the order of the day, much to the relief of James. Teach an optical skill he could do… but a C-section? Not likely!

With the midwife now running the show, James was ready to bring Baby Gibbins number five into the world. Seeing the baby crowning, his excitement nearly took over, but taking a deep breath along with his amazing wife, James guided his new baby into the world. The crowning process done, it was now time for James to catch a glimpse of his new son or daughter's face through the amniotic sac before they slid out into the world into his hands. He had done it! He had delivered their baby, and much to Annie's delight, baby number five was a little girl just as she had hoped for.

Exhausted and exhilarated all at the same time, and now determined to get the vasectomy, James held his new born baby daughter Chelsea in his arms and allowed the build-up of emotions to spread across his face in one of the biggest smiles Annie had ever seen. Falling in love with him on an even deeper level had not seemed possible but here she was spent from a natural labour totally in awe of her hunky husband the midwife. Their family really was now complete, and what a way to complete it!

Returning to their beautiful home, all the children were happy to meet their new baby sister, especially Hannah. She was now a big sister, a role she relished. With all the children doing their bit, and James making time for the boys to have 'boy time' and taking Hannah on 'Daddy dates', family life was better than ever. Each child got their own one-on-one time with each parent and there was never a feeling of ever being left out just because a new baby had arrived. The older children tried to help and Annie made time to go to Hannah's dance classes with her and enjoy precious mother and daughter alone time; memories both of them would always treasure.

Thirty-two, five children and a husband, not to mention a beautiful home, you would think Annie would be contented; but there was a frustration building, and like most stay-at-home mums, Annie wanted more than just conversations about babies, or conversations with small children. She wasn't suffering from post-natal depression, although many today would say she was, she was just frustrated. She wanted to put her brilliant mind to work, was becoming increasingly creative and very motivated. She wanted to return to work and was contemplating studying again, and as she was beginning to realise, anything she puts her mind to, she normally goes on to achieve it… even if it hadn't always been easy or straight forward.

With Chelsea reaching her first birthday, Annie had returned to work at the hospital, and yet the frustration Annie had been feeling was growing stronger. Seeing people coming and going in the hospital, both as patients and medical staff, Annie knew there was more to life than sleeping, taking care or the family and working in a job you enjoyed, but didn't love. Doing her best to resuscitate patients, with many of them too far gone to survive, or watching others left with critical injuries or illnesses, Annie was really beginning to understand just how precious life truly was; and she knew she didn't want to waste her life or live with regrets.

After a particularly difficult day at the hospital, and a lack of sleep the night before, Annie was approached by a distressed Samuel who kept moaning of stomach-ache. Giving him the once over Annie was sure her son was showing signs of appendicitis, and so headed straight for Mona Vale Hospital.

With Samuel admitted and examinations complete, the doctors were not sure what was wrong and wanted to keep him in overnight. Annie's instinct told her otherwise and pressed the doctors to 'do something'. With the doctor on duty looking down his nose at her, a woman who was just a part-time nurse and over-anxious mother, Annie's certainty of appendicitis was growing however the specialist put Samuel in an isolation room with suspected food poisoning for seven days, adamant that she was wrong.

Annie may have been only a part-time nurse, but she had learnt a lot in her short medical career, and besides that, she knew her son was deteriorating and her instinct was telling her to remove her son from Mona Vale and head to Westmead Children's Hospital on the other side of town. Grabbing Samuel and discharging him from hospital care she was warned of the consequences by surprised doctors and nurses; but she didn't care. She had to trust her instincts and thank goodness she did because on arrival at Westmead, Samuel was rushed into emergency surgery due to a ruptured appendix.

With a severe case of peritonitis, Samuel underwent two lots of surgery and was lucky he didn't need a colostomy procedure. He spent five weeks in hospital before being discharged, and on his return home, Annie was met by Caleb who also wasn't feeling very well. A quick examination, and Annie wasn't sure whether to laugh or cry. After instructing James what was happening, Annie jumped back in the car and drove to Royal North Shore hospital with her eldest son and another case of appendicitis. At least he was home again in three days.

A part time nurse she may be, but Annie's quick thinking and trusting her intuition had just saved the lives of two of her children. It was a lot to take in and a lot to process, and with the previous levels of frustration Annie's emotions would soon get the better of her.

Feeling sombre and in need of a boost, another getaway was just what was needed. James' sister had a place at Nelson Bay so it was decided a mini break was on the cards. With bags packed and the kids excited they all set off. It didn't matter that it wasn't the height of summer, a getaway to ease the pressure was needed.

One morning whilst the kids were settled in the front room entertaining themselves and James and Annie were having their morning shower, the smell of smoke started to infiltrate the air. Eyes wide open, staring at each other processing this new piece of aromatic information, they both made a run for the front room where the children were sitting next to an overturned bar heater and flaming curtains. Grabbing the children, fighting the fire and calling the emergency services were all tackled on auto-pilot, so much so Annie had not even given a thought to grabbing her undies and protecting her modesty in the process; something which would raise a few eyebrows many years down the line.

With the children safe, fire out and damage assessed, Annie and James held each other in their arms and stood there. The need to feel safe in each other's arms, to feel held was paramount. Life had been one crazy ride so far and they were still only just beginning. Annie had already amassed a huge amount of experiences and knowledge, been through so much. Surely there wasn't any more to go through. Surely this all meant something, other than proving just what an incredibly strong and courageous woman she was; because like the saying goes "God doesn't give you more than you can handle", and Annie had handled a lot.

Returning back home to Allambie Heights, life resumed as normal with work and school taking up most of the hours in the day. Annie was back at work pretty much full time and all the children were now in either day care or at school; life was good, but still there was a sadness creeping up inside of Annie. One night after a particularly busy day, James noticed Annie was quieter than usual. The kids were in bed and they were alone. One by one tears started to fall, and Annie finally had a meltdown. "I love you, I love the kids, but am I really going to be a nurse forever? Is this my life now? I don't have a social life to even think of now, and I know I am worth more than this. I know I am."

James listened to his wife share all her frustrations, thoughts and feelings, allowing her to process it all. Next to her father, he was her rock. Once the emotions and the frustrations had been released, he simply asked her, "So what do you want?"

Annie didn't know anymore. She thought back to the days she would tell her father she would run the family business, that she would one day run the company, but with a family to think about how would she even find the time to do that?

A few days passed, ideas floated around in her mind, she struck upon the idea of becoming a nursing teacher. James was already studying on top of his work and still able to be a hands-on dad, so why couldn't she do the same? With a big beaming smile on her face, the light shining from deep within her, the high-level energy had returned with gusto as she declared to James, "Right! I am going to go back to university and become a teacher!"

James was not in the slightest bit surprised and told her, "If that's what you want to do, then we'll figure it out."

With this new level of excitement and her curiosity peaking Annie was led back to university to do a Graduate Diploma of Education. She had worked out that with her nursing experience, and this diploma, she would soon be able to become a nursing teacher. With a couple of nights each week at university, away from the kids, Annie found herself enjoying her own company and her own time again. She loved uni life and soon discovered that although she hadn't previously thought of herself as academic, she was really starting to enjoy the learning process, and found out she was really quite good at it.

She also discovered her own 'loop-hole' in the learning process, one which meant if she left home a little earlier than usual, she had time to read a magazine in the café before class. It became her guilty secret and she had her first real insight into what self-care truly was. Annie had started to realise she and James needed time alone when he whisked her off for the mini getaway following the 'sewerage incident'. While initial thoughts felt somewhat luxurious, thoughts had started to percolate on the need to take more care of herself, this time for her to study, to read a magazine alone in a café… this was the insight she needed to set fire to a whole new chain reaction of discovery, even to the point where she started to encourage other women to "Take time out for yourself! It's AMAZING!".

Not all women understood it, or wanted to, but for Annie, time out for herself had been the very thing her soul had been calling out for all along, and now she had answered her own prayers. She had started to gift herself the care and attention she so deserved and needed, the kind of care and attention that couldn't come from anyone else but her, no matter how much others like James, the children or her dad tried. This was a level of care that could only be given to self, and she had discovered it, now there was no holding her back.

Then the 'Mama Guilt' set in when she started imagining how much easier it would be if she only had one child to take care of, if she hadn't had two sets of twins and then got pregnant again. Quickly snapping herself out of her own pity party, she knew there was no point in comparing her life to anyone else's or imaging her life was different in any way. Her life was her life and it was up to her to make the very best out of it, regardless of whatever the circumstances were now and in the future. She was in charge of her own future and she got to decide what was possible, turning the perceived 'impossible' options into the 'I am possible!'.

This was going to be easier said than done though. As with all personal journeys that spark of new motivation needed embodying to become the new normal way of being, and the 'Mama Guilt' had to disappear, especially given the fact that both sets of twins had their mum at home with them playing, cooking together five nights out of seven. Add to this all the involvement Annie had with the children when it came to helping them with homework, being the first to volunteer as the ideal candidate for the various school trips due to being a nurse and able to assist if there were any accidents. Then there were the after-school clubs, the cuddles and encouragement all underpinned with the deep faith in God, a faith in action rather than simply repeating scripture. Living the faith, being the faith and exploring the teachings was encouraged without being dictatorial or fiercely enforced. The more questions the children asked the more answers the whole family sought out together.

This example of exploring answers and asking great questions was also demonstrated to the children by Annie during her study sessions. Seeing their mother study was the incentive they needed to do their own homework, and the excitement of completing an assignment or getting a great grade passed on to all the children, especially Caleb who, being most like his mum than any of his siblings, he watched with a keen interest.

Letting go of the 'Mama Guilt' took time, and the more Annie learnt, the more she saw was possible, even if others in her space thought she was crazy, or unsatisfied, needing to fill a hole within herself. The truth was, the more she learnt, the more she wanted to learn, because the more she learnt, the more people she could help, and the more people she helped, the more lives she could save and the happier everyone was: the patients, the families and the medical teams within the hospital. It was a ripple effect that inspired and encouraged Annie to be more than she ever thought possible, to do more interesting things at work and at home, as well as to have more positive experiences impacting herself, her family and the lives of others.

For Annie it was becoming more apparent that the more we wish to serve others, the more we have to serve ourselves first, and that would take balance and some more fine tuning of what would soon become known as her 'higher level managerial skills' and provide the family with more than a few giggles along the way.

One day you will stop doubting my higher-level managerial skills!

Chapter Thirteen
BECOMING A MASTER

With so many things to juggle and the precise planning and logistical challenges, Annie proved herself more than capable of handling whatever life throws at her; and she had done most of it without the support and encouragement of her mum, the female role model so many women look to in their lives. Managing so many aspects in her personal life was gifting Annie everything she would need as she put her newfound knowledge from studying into practice. Annie was thriving, and so were the nurses she was teaching. It was inevitable that they would all succeed due to the tenacity and joy Annie brought to each lesson, not to mention the unique perspectives she had gained throughout her own life with the curve balls sent her way. Combining all of these elements with the leadership and care she had picked up from her father as he dealt with the customers in the pharmacy every day, there was no way Annie would fail at whatever she chose to do; provided she stayed curious and came with more ideas about what was possible.

Although Annie had never believed herself to be a great student, she was very good at observing the behaviours of others. A quick learner with a big heart, with huge amounts of compassion and empathy for others, Annie was destined for greatness, and her success as a Teacher of Nursing was all the confirmation she needed.

Life had changed in many ways, and not just in family and work matters. Annie was getting interested in sport and entered a Netball competition, started going to the gym more and even took up boxing classes. The more Annie achieved in one area of life, the more she started achieving in other areas of life. It was a knock-on effect that became a way of life, so much so it was inspiring James to up his game. The couple had always been individually competitive, and they used this to spur each other on. Whether it was James pushing her to the rescue of injured souls at the scene of an accident, or whether it was the cheeky rivalry they used to nudge each other forward in their careers, the couple always found a way to inspire, support and encourage each other to be the very best version of self; and in a home environment like that, how could it not rub off on their children?

Annie knew her stuff when it came to taking care of people and was now really starting to take care of herself on a whole new level. Her confidence in standing her ground when it came to medical matters was also being put to the test, especially on one particular holiday when Annie and James were witness to a horse-riding incident whereby a young man was thrown from his horse. His grandfather, a seasoned horseman didn't think too much of it and kept saying, "The boy would be alright." Except Annie knew the 'boy' had broken his collarbone and had a severe neck injury. The grandfather refused to admit it, and it wasn't until the paramedics arrived and confirmed Annie's diagnosis that the grandfather relented.

She didn't get it right all the time though, and sometimes didn't quite understand that when a passenger involved in a car crash told her he couldn't see, it didn't matter how many times she reassured him that it would be alright, the ambulances were on their way, he still wouldn't be able to see because he was blind before the crash. It was in these moments that Annie's warmth and self-deprecating humour brought peace to those around her and resulted in her being loved by so many, regardless of whether it was the first time of meeting or years of friendship.

Sadly, the more Annie succeeded and the more confidence she gained in herself, the more she challenged her mother, and the more women in her life saw her as 'lucky' or 'Super Mum'. These labels sat uncomfortably with Annie, especially as she was putting her natural curiosity, drive and talent to good use. Annie was working hard and incredibly smart for everything she was achieving and made informed choices whilst also listening to her own intuition. She believed in herself, and she wanted to see what was possible. She was no different to any other woman who made the choice to apply herself and get curious. She was simply being herself, doing what she wanted and being supported by her husband, a husband she chose, and had a marriage which they both invested in. She had personal challenges just like anyone else, family health scares, and more baggage than most to deal with. The memories of what her brother did all those years back, and his friends at the party still visited Annie whenever she walked past the location or went into certain parts of her parent's family home. The man she had loved all her life was dying a slow death from a brain tumour, watching his surviving each day was heart breaking in many ways, but none of the challenges were going to stop Annie from going after what she wanted.

A couple of years after Annie completed her graduate diploma, she realised that she wanted to start studying again. With so many things she had been told she couldn't do, or wouldn't be able to do being proved wrong, Annie started to question everything she had ever believed about what was possible, not just for her, but for other women too. With the new question in her mind of, *What if this isn't true?* Annie started to set her sights on bigger and bigger things. Her dad may have told her once that she couldn't run a business because of the children taking up all her time, but she had been holding down a nursing career, studying AND taking care of the family, so what else was possible?

Having got curious about what was possible, Annie came up with the idea of doing a Master of Education. James was as supportive as ever and the children were never surprised with the ideas their mother came up with, it was 'just Mum doing what Mum does'. Life had improved a lot since both Annie and James had become teachers. More of life's luxuries, more time with the children, better clothes, nicer cars and better presents for the kids on their birthdays. As the older kids grew up they noticed their younger sister Chelsea was benefiting from international travel with Mum and Dad, but Annie just responded with yes but how blessed were you to have so much more 'Mumma Time'.

Not that the lifestyle differences mattered to any of the children, they all had a set of fun-loving parents who supported them in whatever it was they wanted to do. School trips were encouraged, as was travel, and although neither parent was pushy, they made sure the children explored all the options available; just like Annie had when applying for her Masters.

When she told her colleagues at TAFE she was going to complete a Masters, a couple of the senior staff told her she was crazy. They expressed it wasn't necessary for her job, would cost lots of money, she already had her dream job for life, and it would take time away from her 'Mummy duties'. The words 'dream job for life' were not what she wanted to hear, because the more she explored the possibilities of having a Master of Education, the more excited she became, and when Annie gets excited, there is no stopping her and the momentum that takes hold.

With the news of more study, more trouble was caused with her own mother, but by now Annie had more than learnt not to take any notice, even though it still hurt her deep down. Even though many people thought she was taking on too much, she did it anyway and loved it even more than the previous degree.

The unexpected bonus of the Masters was that she got to meet so many interesting people from different cultures and careers, which reminded her of her own grandmothers and their life journeys, not to mention all the homestay guests she and James had welcomed into their home over the years.

Having already relished her guilty secret of a loophole of 'me time' years before, the two nights away from the kids each week was a nice break. The kids were growing up and becoming independent, learning to voice their own opinions and stand their ground. With the after-school clubs, school trips and sibling rivalry, two nights all to herself away from it all was blissful.

Annie's great sense of humour didn't just fuel laughter in the home, but it also allowed the children to be at ease with her. Annie and James had created a loving home where everyone was free to express themselves and grow in confidence in everything they chose to do. So when Annie started to walk around the house repeating, "I know you think I'm just your mummy but I do have high level managerial skills you know, and one day I'm going to be a business woman. Just you watch!"

The children would giggle and say, "Sure Mum, whatever you say," and continue on with their days.

Undeterred and a 'pioneer of vision boards' Annie put a note on the fridge saying: "Mum has high level managerial skills" just to remind herself, and everyone in the home just what she was made of.

Loving what she was doing and seeing how far she could go would raise the question of "Why are you not content with what you have?". Wanting to see what her full potential was had nothing to do with being content or discontented, it was just a fascinating process and the more she learnt, the more she realised she had to learn. Every step she took, the more she learnt about what was possible, and her vision for the future evolved. It had nothing to do with ego either, just a curious nature of wanting to know if we ever reach our full potential.

Annie was most definitely the driver in the family when it came to understanding and pursuing potential, however the family income was not the priority as long as they were all happy and willing to do their best in whatever they chose to do.

All five children were vastly different, even each twin to the other. Caleb was always pushing himself to the next level like his mum, whilst Daniel and his younger brother Samuel were more relaxed about life; Hannah wanted to take to the stage and teach just like her mum and Chelsea was the deep thinker of the family. Each had their own challenges in life and always knew no matter what was going on with their parents work or study, everything would stop for them when they really needed their parents. It also didn't matter what others said or projected onto Annie about her drive and enthusiasm for achieving more because she knew the kind of mother she was, and she knew what it felt like not to have a mother's support; and there was no way her children would feel the way she had when growing up.

With the hours of study needed to complete her Masters, the children would see their mum reading and completing assignments and getting excited about stationery. With post-it notes, journals and pens in a variety of colours, each for a different project or task type, the children were learning how to study and apply themselves. They didn't need telling, they just followed their mother's lead.

With her Master of Education completed in 2008, Annie applied for the National Education Manager job with the Orthopaedic Surgeons. It was a big deal and with it being the first and only application she sent off Annie was just testing the waters. The job came with a massive salary increase and would mean great things for the family, more travel for one thing; but would she get it? Would Annie be able to prove her theory of becoming a businesswoman one day? Did she really have the potential to lead others and a business to success? The confirmation that she did have what it took came when the job became hers and her high-level managerial skills became more than a note on the fridge and cheeky banter between friends and family. Now she could say with complete confidence and a sparkle in her eyes that she did indeed have high-level managerial skills… and was about to buy the t-shirt and wear it!

You were born to be you so embrace your evolution

Chapter Fourteen
BECOMING INSPIRED

Wearing the t-shirt of life adventures, and misadventures is one of those phrases in life many of us have come accustomed to hearing, along with the all-time favourite of those wishing to keep others small. You'll know the one, about the station and getting ideas above it. Annie had first heard it from her dad when he told her she wasn't good enough at maths to become a businesswoman, and how she had to stay home and take care of the children. Being told not to 'get ideas above our station' can be delivered in a plethora of different ways, and yet we are never really told what station we are at, or what kind of station it is. Like many things from our families, these phrases are passed down from generation to generation, and we as individuals are left to choose what we take on board, and what we leave behind, another great phrase and analogy of life.

Learning more about both of her grandmothers was a turning point for Annie, and a key piece of understanding in the relationship with her mother. Her grandmothers were one of the strongest influences in her life, and the gift of strength, resilience and independence was one of the greatest gifts to have been passed down the generations.

On one side of Annie's family you had Irene Volkov, the mother of Annie's mum. She was born in Moscow, Russia, as Baroness De Schultz, daughter of Baron de Schultz, an officer in the Russian Navy. A lofty title and one of breeding, which during the Russian Revolution of 1917 wouldn't mean much for very long, especially as two revolutions swept through the country. These revolutions would mean the end to centuries of imperial rule and bring about political and social reform, bringing the Soviet Union into fruition.

It wasn't just a time of great unrest for Annie's grandmother and great grandfather, especially as Russia was one of the most impoverished countries in Europe at the time, with a vast number of peasants and an increasing number of poor industrial workers. Russia was viewed as an 'under-developed, backward society' by most of the world, not just by Western Europe. It was the 'Black sheep of the European family, and it was during the practiced serfdom of The Russian Empire that landless peasants we forced to serve the land-owning nobility, of which Irene, Annie's grandmother, was one of.

Not that this really accounted for much, because when Irene was just eight years old, the typhus plague hit her hometown, killing both her mother and sister. They were among the three million civilians killed by typhus between the years of 1918 and 1922.

With politics being as they were, it was surprising to find Annie's great grandfather sent her grandmother to Germany via a network of Jewish friends to be raised by his sister Nellie and her governess Emma.

Moving to Paris at the age of 18, meeting the man of her dreams, who she wanted to practice medicine with, was an incredible achievement during those years. Sadly, due to the way social classes held tight to titles and positioning within society, their marriage wasn't allowed. The loss of her title as Baroness, and no longer being of 'the right class' of people, Irene was also made to do nursing instead of medicine. She was devastated, but she wasn't going to be stopped in her drive and ambition. Irene spoke five languages, which allowed her to live her life in relative comfort and connect with many different people, always impressing those whom she met.

The more Annie learnt about her grandmother the more similarities and connections she saw and felt. The titles stripped away, didn't stop her, akin to the dreams dashed by Annie's mother. The social discrimination of the German elite, no different to the social discrimination of the bullying Annie experienced in the playground at high school; same meat, just a very different flavour and gravy to disguise it all.

Learning about her dad's mum, Mary Montgomery, brought even more insights into how powerful behaviours and attitudes get passed on from generation to generation. Mary was a self-made woman and true survivor, an independent little madam in some people's point of view. There were no lofty titles, or society breeding here with Mary, but the sense of adventure and a fierce independence written into DNA which would get passed down to Annie in abundance.

At the young age of two years old, Mary and her brother were left in the care of their grandmother when their mother ran off to New Zealand with a new lover. Now being left with your grandmother may sound like a great blessing to many but being treated like a servant and refused any and all opportunities, and certainly not the sweet-smelling home of jam tarts and hot coco cuddles one would imagine.

Although life was tough, Mary met a guy, fell in love and settled down, becoming a mother to three lively children. Sadly, this marriage was not to last, and Annie's grandfather divorced her grandmother, leaving her to raise the three children alone. With social attitudes being what they were in the 1950s this was a harder job than it is today, even though not much has changed all that much in the way in which single mothers are looked upon and treated. Openly frowned upon, the one who must be at fault, single mums in the 1950s set the stage for the women of today to be fiercely independent and resourceful; and Mary had both of these attributes in abundance.

Going back to night school to study accountancy, Mary was changing the game for generations of women to come. Very few women were accepted for any subject in business other than secretarial duties, but this did not deter Mary, nor did the exhaustion she felt of being single mum by day, student by night. Graduating and becoming an accountant made the late nights and early mornings all worth it, especially when her workaholic nature led her to owning her own property, a unit she could call her own. Mary's dedication to her work and the strong leadership qualities she possessed kept her working until her retirement age of 76, some 16 years longer than most women today.

With such great female role models as grandmothers, women whom Annie loved to bits, there is no wonder Annie had high aspirations to make her way in the world as a businesswoman. The resilience shown to Annie both intentionally and subconsciously by these pioneering women was powerful, and in times of wondering what was possible, Annie would ask herself, "If they could achieve all this back then in their day, then what can I achieve?"

The fact that both grandmothers did it alone and had shown Annie what was truly possible with a spot of elbow grease and determination, there was no way Annie being Annie wouldn't allow her imagination to run riot and go off on a wild and crazy adventure of what was possible for her; and her family. The biggest differences for Annie were she had the support of her loving husband James, and a new way of thinking in the world of business. Women were no longer 'just the secretary' or a piece of 'eye candy' for bosses to look at, or even a 'backside to slap and ogle' as she walked through the office space, women were in business to do business, be in charge of the business, and Annie was in the right place at the right time.

As with everything though, you can be in the right place at the right time and nothing great happens, and nor is it about luck of the draw. Annie was seeing opportunities in front of her, asking the right questions of herself, and getting deep down and dirty with her own potential. What was really possible for her? What was the most outrageous thing she could achieve right now?

Looking back over her life, there were some pretty outrageous things which had happened for her, and although she may not have understood them at the time, the lows had brought with them the resilience she had inherited from her grandmothers.

With her diverse heritage, the curse of typhus which not only claimed the lives of her grandmother Irene's mother and sister, but also her great grandpa, who added to the diversity by bringing in some Swiss culture, Annie's blood line was impressing on her more lessons and insights that would catapult her even further than she could ever imagine.

Learning about her grandfather who worked as an architect, and his fatal love affair with drink post World War II, also pressed upon Annie the need to make wise choices when it came to balance and resolving the underlying issues which will always haunt us if not dealt with.

The issues with her mum were still very much unresolved but, understanding more about who her grandmothers were, and the more her own journey of motherhood unfolded, Annie was learning to resolve her own issues; learning to really tap into the teachings in the bible of forgiveness, even if it stung like a bee sometimes.

During a rare occasion of mother-daughter bonding at a Jewish museum, Annie's mum pointed to a hat and told her, "I have a hat just like that at home from my grandfather." Annie couldn't quite believe it, her grandfather was Jewish? Why was she previously unaware of this Jewish history? But the more the story unfolded, the more Annie realised the challenges of race and diversity her mother had experienced. When her mother came to Australia from France age 12 with no English, she was teased and bullied at school for being a WOG. Understandably, this made her resentful of who she was, especially when it was never addressed, simply brushed under the carpet and left to fester.

Motherhood being the interesting journey it is, with a vast array of different mother-daughter dynamics, Annie was really getting to grips with how important it was to do her best to work things out with her mum. Watching, learning and experiencing what it meant to be part of the healing process for patients in the hospital, combined with the new knowledge Annie was learning with her Masters of Education, Annie knew the best way to lead her children was to lead by example.

To be the best version of herself meant all aspects of her life, and her first priority above all else was to make time for family when they needed her, regardless of what was going on. With five children, all incredibly different, with their own unique set of gifts and challenges, Annie was getting an insight into what it must have been like for her grandmothers. They may have been single, as opposed to Annie being married, but sometimes even with James by her side the challenges of motherhood and work became too much. Emotions would get the better of her, tiredness would set in and yet underneath it all was the ability to be grateful, discovering more gratitude and solutions with her incessant curiosity.

With her mother's choice to spend more time with her grandsons rather than her granddaughters, the complexities and distance between Annie and her mother deepened. The Mama Fire within Annie would rise to protect her children from spiteful comments, favouritism, and as always James would step in as the ever-diplomatic peacekeeper, or at least try to be. Playing the peacekeeper between any two women is no easy task, especially for a man who is husband to one and son-in-law to the other; but with his tenacity and charm, James would always eventually manage to moderate the situations presented.

With time to reflect upon all she was learning about her grandmothers, the childhood memories and the words of wisdom they gifted her, Annie was more in awe of them then she had ever been. When she received an intended insult from her mum of, "You're just like your grandmother!" Annie was delighted! Being told she was just like Mama was one of the biggest compliments her mother ever paid her and left Annie feeling a childlike rebellion, not to mention a sense of optimism and excitement knowing she was destined for greatness.

More inspiration was being presented to Annie by James and each of their children as they presented her with a very different view of life, and of the vast array of health issues they faced. By now Annie was more than aware of the restrictions of foods James could eat, and the emergency responses needed when it came to his peanut allergy. She had learnt to recognise and deal with her own asthma attacks, although at times she liked to push herself a little bit too hard, and not be 'delicate' about the situations that occurred. With the peanut allergy and Annie's asthma attack, mission aid work to Thailand was curtailed, meaning a lot of previous dreams slipped away. With Annie always being the one to take care of others, and not have a fuss made of her, James would sometimes have to put his *foot down with a firm hand* and remind Annie to rest and take care of herself.

All great advice but when your children need you, it is always time to crank it up a gear. As with most mothers, when you think you are performing at your highest capacity, you always find reserves in the tank to take care of your child, especially when a health scare grips your child in physical, emotional and mental capacities. Being one of five children, there was a little bit of pressure to not be the 'whiney one' along with a little bit of teasing and sibling rivalry. In the Gibbins family, the sibling rivalry was beautifully balanced with love and support, and with six other people in the family, everyone had one of the biggest cheerleading squads of many of their friends. The children also knew regardless of their views on life, religion and social issues, their individual ideas and goals would all be encouraged, with both Annie and James seeking out information, application forms and solutions to help make things happen, and not in a pushy way, although with Caleb, a little more push would have been preferred.

With all this love, support and encouragement, when Hannah suffered from a severe medical condition and was taken into hospital, Annie was by her side throughout. The family rallied round, and everyone stepped up to the mark. With dark thoughts, depression, anxiety and panic attacks gripping Hannah, knowing her mum was by her side, and the love from her dad, brothers and sister was all the light she needed to bring her out of the darkness.

It didn't matter what time Annie had to wake up to get all her work done so she could drive to the hospital to be with Hannah, if that is what was needed to be done, then that is what would be done. With James as the second in command and calling on an army of helpers, there was little disruption to the rest of the family and homelife carried on as normal, well as normal as life can without the high level managerial skills and constant chatter of the effervescent Annie at the helm.

Watching their mum manage so many projects at once, each child was picking up on a vast array of capabilities and resilience which would go on to serve them all well in later life. Her fun and vibrant energy would brighten up every situation, including conversations about the ongoing health of her dad and his grossly misjudged time left on the planet. According to doctors he should have died many years before, but he was now very much into extra time and penalties.

Annie's desire to trouble shoot the regular and predictable sibling disputes were resolved quickly and without too much drama.

Watching their mum interact with friends when on school trips, the Gibbins children would feel immense pride, and sometimes a little sprinkling of embarrassment when they heard their mum discussing subjects such as periods with the girls, and the sense of amazement whenever she sprang into action as Nurse Annie. When school trips were at an end, and questions of what to get their 'super cool mum' as a thank you gift came up, there was never really an answer. Annie never did anything for gifts or recognition, she just wanted the girls to know there is a princess inside all of us, and for the boys to feel heard and respected. Watching how Annie would give all of herself to their peers at school, and to those in need of medical care, would instil in the children the gift of giving to others, of selflessness. Watching how their mum would always treat people kindly, and not speak ill of people, treating each person with the individual respect and value, were some of the most inspiring moments and diplomatic life lessons for the young teenagers.

The inspiration didn't stop there though. With the number of things going on career wise for both James and Annie, it was time for a holiday, and with the world to explore it was destination Europe. Why not? It was doable, it would be the European adventure Annie and James had promised the kids 10 years prior 'if they were good'. Now when you are new parents, you get given a lot of advice and insights, and it was one particular word of warning they had been given when the twins were three and five that led to a bold commitment. Hearing the words 'you had better enjoy them now as you are going to have four teenagers!' felt a future nightmare was looming so to inspire rather than bribe, they told the kids that for the next 10 years if they were good they would be taken to Europe.

A Europe fund was started and every time they did a job money got paid into it. The best decision they ever made because not only did it teach the kids the start of how to be financially intelligent, it was also time to call in that Europe Fund, which had generated more than a few ice creams each that was for sure! Packed lunches, homestays, and staying with friends made whilst Annie and James had been homestay hosts themselves, the whole family were getting excited. How could they not? They were going to be exploring London, Switzerland, Germany and Italy. To make things more interesting, instead of choosing together where to stay, Annie and James came up with the plan of alternating who chose the next location. James was a lot more frugal with the spending than Annie, and the idea of *real* camping wasn't exciting Annie in the slightest. There were no lunches out in restaurants, just simple family picnics in the parks and plazas, with scenes reminiscent of the Von Trapp family.

In Germany they stayed with their beloved homestay student Andrea who now had two sons and owned a farm stay resort with her husband and in Switzerland it was time to visit their homestay friend Benedict. Having never met Hannah, Samuel or Chelsea, and having last seen

Caleb and Daniel as babies, it was time for looks of confusion from the kids and startled looks from Benedict. Fifteen years had passed, and with two 15-year-olds, two 13-year-olds and a seven-year-old, the home was soon filled with stories and fond memories around the discovery of twins and then more twins, before the fear of triplets but the hope of a daughter none the less.

To the surprise of Annie and James, Benedict had arranged a night away at a local hotel for the two of them while his family minded their kids. A seven-week holiday around Europe with just a couple of children would have been hectic, but five! A little time out for both the parents and the children was a necessity, much like the time away by themselves all those years before when their first home in Allambie heights was flooded. Time out does everyone good, and this was the rejuvenation they all needed before the next leg of their trip, and their return home, which wouldn't be home for much longer.

Refreshed and recharged from the trip it was nice to be back home. Having sold the home they had built together five years earlier, they had found the perfect family home in Davidson, a leafy suburb, full of young families and safe cul-de-sacs to play in. It had also been the perfect place to find space in heart and mind as they came to terms with the news about Annie's dad's brain tumour. It seemed with every house move Annie and James embarked up, it would bring with it the added challenges.

First they moved from Allambie due to unwanted gifts from the sewerage system, and in the process of building what they believed would be the family home for many years to come they were blessed with Chelsea; and at the time of the move to Davidson they were given the news Annie's father had only six to 12 months to live. The Davidson home felt like home, and having lived on the western edge of the Garigal National Park, it was time for the eastern side. Named after Sir Walter Davidson, the Governor of New South Wales during 1918 to 1923, Davidson was a mining area until the mid-1970s when it started to become an upmarket residential area. In 1994 part of Davidson was nearly destroyed due to the bushfires that raged in the nearby Garigal National Park, saved only by the brilliant efforts of the Warringah/Pittwater Rural Fire Service.

Together they were becoming quietly unstoppable, as was their love and attraction for one another. James seeing everything his gorgeous wife was achieving couldn't quite believe sometimes just how lucky he was. He had a wife who just kept showing up for herself, him and their children in the most surprising of ways. Always delivering, always shining even when there was so much which could bring her down, Annie always rose above it all, seeing the positives in every negative. It didn't matter what seemed to be going on in their own lives, Annie was always there to help others who needed it, proving the old adage that if you want something done, ask a busy woman!

*I'm a lover
not a fighter,
with a
side serve of feisty*

Chapter Fifteen

SNAPSHOTS OF LIFE

Annie and James on their wedding day, together signing the register

Above: Annie with the first love of her life on her wedding day, her dad Mr Montgomery

Above: Annie's grandmothers Mary (left next to James) and Irene (right next to Annie)

Back row L-R: James with baby Chelsea just a few months old, Annie and Caleb
Front row L-R: Daniel, Samuel and Hannah

Above: The 'hunky husband' and 'gorgeous wife' climbing a different kind of mountain together

Above: Climbing to the top in all areas of life is a challenge Annie grasps with great focus and agility

Below: Finding balance of a different kind, above the ocean in 2017

Right: Annie with His Excellency Mr David Hurley, Governor General and his wife Mrs Hurley

Left: Raising awareness for Glaucoma Australia on stage; and

Below: With Kirk Pengilly, INXS band member, on Sunrise TV

Learning to say no is life changing

Chapter Sixteen

BECOMING SMARTER

Embodying the attitude of simply going for it, even if it feels daunting or mistakes are made along the way, was the perseverance that made all the difference. Many times over the years, Annie's asthma provided her with life threatening situations that worried both the doctors and James, but Annie was quick to recover and take the attention away from what had happened and look at the next exciting opportunity.

With the knowledge learnt and implemented from her master's degree, Annie's role of National Education Manager for the Australian Orthopaedics Association was both enjoyable and an awakening of what was really possible, and not just within the framework of the human body.

Formed in 1937 when the founding members assigned Edward Vance as its very first elected President, it has served a great number of trainees and surgeons with exceptional training and development, saving many people from pain and immobility in the process, and gifting them freedom to move and be independent.

Watching how the organisation of 1700 surgeons organised itself, developed the future surgeons, and shared information with the public on all things orthopaedic, Annie's mind was having a party of the neurons. Understanding the mobility of the body from the musculoskeletal and nervous systems angle was intriguing to say the least; and knowing the freedom and ease of movement was given back to a great many patients through the education delivered by the association was incredibly satisfying, especially given as it was her job to deliver, train and develop first class educational programmes for the trainee orthopaedic surgeons across Australia.

It was never just the textbooks which Annie learnt from, it was watching people in action, listening to conversations, the words spoken, and the words unspoken. Working alongside so many brilliant, and gifted surgeons simulated an executive crash course in leadership. Coupled with travelling around the world with the children, to life learnings were now on speed dial.

It didn't really matter where in the world Annie was because being in nature would lift her spirits and fill her heart with serenity. Being in God's garden was the escape from all things upsetting, such as the continued ill health of her father, and the ongoing saga with her mother. Having been told over a decade ago her dad only had six to 12 months to live was a cruel curse in many ways. Not knowing would have been kinder, but working in the medical field, Annie had the professional insight to understand why they had been told, even though on a personal level it was knowledge she wished she didn't have.

The upside of knowing, and her dad still being around to watch his grandchildren grow up into young adults, meant each day was appreciated more than ever; but in all reality, how could that even be measured? Having been given a 'death sentence' by the doctors obviously wasn't something Annie's dad was going to listen to, and a reminder for Annie that she was like her father in so many ways, stubborn, unlikely to do what others told them to do and a passion for life that was going to be lived on their own terms This didn't stop the worry in the deep subconscious mind of Annie, James and the famous five named Gibbins. Watching, wondering, worrying whether it would be today, this week, month or year was deeply upsetting, but it was a waiting game that everyone had to play, even if they didn't know how to at times.

When Annie's mind wasn't thinking about the most exciting and ridiculous things she could achieve next in her career, her mind would turn attention to helping others on a much larger scale, but as always, it was family first.

Showing an interest in everyone and everything, asking others about their hobbies, interests, careers, and the things that got them excited was one of the things her daughter Hannah really admires about her. On one of Annie's many volunteering roles as the designated First Aider, Hannah and Annie were off to Japan for an elite dance tour, part of the extracurricular programme for Hannah's study programme in school. Dance had huge appeal for Hannah, a way to express oneself, to tell stories through each and every move, the costumes, the backdrops, and the music. Her spirit lifted each time she took part or watched a beautiful performance, her face lighting up every time she spoke of it.

The trip to Japan wasn't smooth sailing and many of the young girls were confused and upset about the difference in culture, providing Annie an opportunity to create understanding and peace amongst the girls. 'Being everyone's mum' helped also smooth the path for Hannah and impress upon her how to 'meet people where they are at', one of the many special gifts Annie possessed and passed on to her five children. Having developed a wonderful bedside manner as a nurse, and blessed with a natural gift of making others smile with her quirky, vibrant and energetic self, it was not surprising Annie soon became preferred parent of choice for all school trips scheduled by students and teachers alike.

She knew the time had come to up her game once more so started researching courses and the job market. Having been National Education Manager for five years, Annie had learnt more than a thing or two about the style of course she wanted to do, and which style of course she was looking for. She was also aware of how to complete a training needs analysis on both herself, and future opportunities. They would help her narrow down her search, making her more efficient and wasting less time on the things that didn't matter. With the ideas flowing for Lipstick Consulting, and having had time to search the courses of interest, Annie chose to complete the Australian Institute of Company Directors Course which provided her with all the knowledge she would need for the governance and compliance of a director within Australia, as well as a way to develop her skills as a director for the day that she would eventually become the businesswoman she had told her dad she would become. Whilst she was looking at the variety of courses available, she looked further into Lean Six Sigma, the global standard in process management and profitability. Annie enrolled in completing the Green Belt course and passed with flying colours.

Family life was also changing dramatically as Caleb and Daniel had now completed their HSC, and Caleb ever the focused one in the family, had met, got married and was leaving the family home to begin married life with Beth. Daniel remained at home, with Samuel, Hannah and Chelsea.

Feelings of pressure to perform, and to make sure her mum was proud of her, Hannah started to feel a sense of overwhelm. It never lasted very long and was always easily overcome by having an open and honest conversation with each other. Knowing that finding the right career was never all about the income received for the work they did was a weight off the minds of the five children. James' dream job as a pastor was never about the money, it was about service to others, and so long as the job the children chose was something that made them happy, then both parents were happy. There was no judgement, each person within the family were on their own journey and had to discover for themselves what worked for them; even down to choosing their own individual journey of faith. To believe or not to believe, and which path along the faith did they want to travel was entirely the choice of each individual themselves; and would always provide interesting and insightful conversations.

Annie and James had always been about faith in action rather than simply following the scriptures blindly, and it showed in the mission and aid work they had taken part in over the years. The more Annie learnt about the world of business, the more she would look at the model of religion. Was it all about the theory, or was it about the implementation of ideas? Helping and supporting others, being of service meant businesses stayed in business; it also meant everyone prospered, well when done with the goal of everyone benefitting. Coming from a nursing background, and having been in education in the medical field, it made complete sense that Annie would start to question everything on a holistic basis. Was the actions and message creating ease and ability for all? Was the methodology effective and productive? How was the whole person benefiting? Where were the trigger points, the pain points and what were the solutions to the challenges faced?

Approaching her 40th birthday Annie also started to take stock of everything she had achieved. They say life begins at forty, but if life was only now just beginning what on earth could be achieved now, other than a great party? With the party organised and friends invited, the happy day arrived. Excited to share her home with her friends and celebrate this new beginning, the music was turned up, people were dancing and the noise levels were rising, so much so the police arrived to make sure the noise was turned down. Annie finding this highly amusing, because that's the stuff teenagers have happen to them, was not deterred in her celebrations. The noise was turned down, and the party continued, only to have another knock at the door just over an hour later by the police yet again asking for the noise to be turned down otherwise a noise disturbance order would be issued! Annie couldn't control herself, the laughter was too much, or it had been too much champagne, but here she was this respectful woman turning forty, being told off by the police for having a loud party. Oh, how she would never live this one down!

Looking at everything through the eyes of a CEO, meant that when Annie eventually became one, the transition would be an easy one; the funny thing was though, Annie didn't realise those higher level managerial skills she had so often joked about with the family, were already fully immersed in her very being and becoming a CEO was a natural state of being.

Get out of my lane, I'm coming through at high speed!

Chapter Seventeen
BECOMING CEO

One of the things taught within the personal and professional development field is that before you can do and have things, you actually have to BE the person to be able to receive said opportunities and have said things. If anything was proving Annie would be a successful CEO it was the challenges she'd been through in life, and the impact of facing them all at once. Add to that the grace in which she handled herself throughout all of it, and Annie had everything within her to become CEO of any organisation she chose.

She was most definitely the CEO of the Gibbins family, and fully supported in this role by the wonderfully supportive James, who at times wondered how on earth she managed to remain positive all the time. The thing was though he had created space for her to be all of who she chose to be. He had created a strong foundation of safety for her to flourish, so even though Annie was the driving force behind everything, he was the security she needed to be able to be all of who she was. Annie was safe to take the risks she took because she knew James would be there supporting her, exploring ideas with her and being the rock she needed especially as her dad was still ill and facing the never ending death sentence of the Oligodendroglioma tumour in his brain, a tumour which affects more men than women, and either presents itself as grade 2 type tumour which is present within the body for years without going noticed, or as a grade 3 type which is incredibly aggressive.

For many years, Annie's dad was getting strange muscle seizures in his legs, with his body getting cold with cramps, especially in his hands. He'd get frustrated by being told by doctors there was nothing wrong with him and that it was probably 'in his head', ironically it was, even though he never got a headache. When he finally got seen by a doctor who sent him for a brain scan, the world changed and not just for him, but for Annie too. Here was the man who she had always been eager to please, the man she wanted to prove to that she could become a businesswoman, and she had done it, all whilst being a mother, and he was incredibly proud of her. As her dad's seizures increased, they were being managed by an oncologist, with a brain surgeon completing an 'Awake open craniotomy' to debulk the tumour. His time was running out. The surgery would be able to remove all of the tumour but would affect other parts of the brain. It did affect his memory and coordination over the years, an extremely frustrating aspect of the journey as he was fiercely independent, active and highly intelligent.

For many successful people there is a driver that keeps them striving forward. Many of them are very aware of the reason why, and others are oblivious on a conscious level. Annie was simply curious and inquisitive, and although the desire to prove her dad wrong in the most playful of ways and make him proud of her was a major driving force. The cheeky, rebellious side of Annie was always as play, and with as much love and respect as possible for her dad, she was determined to prove to him she was a businesswoman of the highest calibre. She was going to run a business, and she was going to do it as a CEO!

She wouldn't have long to wait though, especially with the directors course and the Lean Six Sigma under her belt. Annie had already started asking the question of "How on earth did he get the job of CEO?" when a CEO she admired was replaced with another. Her mindset shifted to "What if I could be the CEO of a small heath education association?"

For most people the thought of going from a manager to a regional manager was a big thing, so going from a teacher to national manager to CEO within five years was unthinkable; but Annie did the unthinkable because she believed the only limits are the ones others impose upon you, and well, there are no rules for which jobs you apply for, and if there were, Annie wasn't aware of them, so why not go for the top job? Audacious it might seem to some people, but Annie only saw it as exciting, almost like a game of chance. The 'What if's' were not negatives in Annie's world, they invited opportunities, adventures and possibilities, and there was a big adventure up ahead, and it was going to prove life changing in many ways, and not just for her.

The women in Annie's world were watching, watching how this warm and open hearted woman handled everything life was putting in her path, and still managing to climb the corporate ladder with a smile on her face and more energy than a jack in a box bursting out to surprise you. Being in Annie's space was incredibly inspiring and left many people wondering where on earth all her energy came from. Women were either intrigued or intimidated as to how she always looked amazing and seemed to be defying the ageing process. How did she do it? What was the magic formula? The simple answer to both of these questions was easy, she was just *being* Annie, the woman who had a natural drive to help everyone and anyone, to be their best self, whilst she became her best self.

Getting out in nature as often as possible was essential for Annie, and an act of worship. Having an unwavering belief in releasing whatever she couldn't process, or feel like she couldn't handle, up to God, another act of worship and faith. Trusting everything would work itself out, not stressing about anything also helped with defying the ageing process. Learning to be still, being regular in prayer isn't all about sitting on a yoga mat or kneeling on the ground in front of a cross in church; It is about getting out in nature and appreciating all of God's creations, breathing in the fresh air, exploring the mind, pushing whilst also respecting the body, and connecting with fellow humans.

Over the years Annie had learnt that church was good for those who needed or wanted structure, but not for those who want to be honest and ask questions that challenge the status quo. Annie's faith is based on honesty, openness and being of service to others, forgiving what has gone before, but not forgetting what happened. Remembering has gifted Annie lessons to learn from and is faith in action at its finest. The traditional frameworks of the church were too rigid, and although Annie's faith is stronger than ever, she was beginning to find it hard not to be critical of the church due to her savvy business mind.

Being a believer, a person of faith and service, wasn't about waiting for church on a Sunday or following a scripture to the letter. Faith for Annie meant being fluid, responsive to the needs of others and yourself in any and every given moment. It wasn't about making others fearful, or of judging others of a different faith. It was about learning from each other, supporting and uplifting each other, because when you believe in God and believe He created everyone and everything in the natural world, then how can you not respect those creations? How can you not be of service to others, learn from each other and be respectful?

With all the qualities it took to be a CEO in the bag, Annie has certainly embodied the BEing of a CEO, so now all she had to do to have the official title of CEO was to apply for the job she wanted and get it. Wanting to push and break boundaries wasn't the prime objective for Annie, it was always about seeing what was true and what was possible, combined with what feels right. Being of service to others, helping them see what was truly possible and getting excited by the outcome, another strong driver for Annie. Looking back over her career history it was easy to see the pattern of wanting others to be their best self. Nursing and education are two of the greatest vocations to work in when you are a heart warrior, wanting to serve others and help them become their greatest version of self is at the core of both.

With the intention being set on becoming CEO, Annie started looking for roles which she found interesting. It didn't take her long and she found a job for the CEO of the Australasian Society for Ultrasound in Medicine. They were looking for a Health Educationalist CEO and so she applied. Upon hearing the news, the family were stunned, and not surprised in the slightest. It was just the kind of thing Annie would do, because like she said, "If you didn't have a go, how would you know what you were capable of?" Applying for the job made perfect sense to her.

Not long after applying, Annie was both surprised and delighted to know she had been invited for an interview. The thought of having actually been invited for an interview was one thing, going along to it and then receiving the offer of the job was completely unexpected. Totally stoked and surprised, the next thought to go through Annie's mind was "If this is possible, and it is, WOW! What else is possible?" She hadn't even started the job and was wondering what else was possible!

MAGIC is Achieved when Goals are Intentional and Clear

Chapter Eighteen
BECOMING MAGICAL

With so much going on in everyone's lives, it was hardly surprising that it was now 2010 and 12 years since they had all moved into the Davidson home. Had it really been that long? Well, apparently yes! Hannah and Samuel were in the process of completing their HSC, with Hannah choosing to become a primary school teacher. She was putting her dream of becoming an actress and her love of theatre to one side as she dived into the teaching qualifications with a four-year university course. Samuel took up an apprenticeship at a local bakery and became a baker and pastry chef. The family were in a new stage of preparing for the next big step in their lives. With all of them making huge life choices, the strength of the family foundations built over the years meant no idea or conversation was off the table, and options were explored, ideas listened to and choices respected.

Neither James nor Annie would dream of telling their children what career path to take, especially after the drive and commitment shown by Annie to achieve everything she wanted. Understanding and respecting their children, and their choices meant both parents received the respect of their children in return.

So with exams, career changes, Caleb moving out, getting engaged and married, blink and you would miss it all. Life was changing fast, and sadly life was also evaporating fast.

With her dad's health deteriorating at a slow pace over the years, his struggle getting worse and being unable to care for himself, the Montgomery family home was put up for sale. It had always been a wish that the home remain in the family, and as ever the loyal daughter, Daddy's girl and eager to please her dad, Annie spoke with James about buying it rather than allowing it to go to someone else. He could then move to a retirement village with nursing care nearby and he would be happy that his daughter was enjoying the home he loved for 42 years.

Moving back into the family home would normally bring a lot of joy for most people, but by doing so, Annie was about to embark upon one of the greatest challenges of her life. Memories of her brother raping her in the very home she was about to buy, a home she was buying so she could make her dad happy. His happiness meant more to her than the fear of the torment and trauma she had experienced at the hands of her brother.

Could she really do this?

Flashbacks of the night left alone with her big brother to babysit, telling her about his new camera and how he wanted to test it out, wanted to take photos of her in sexual poses and if she didn't comply she would regret it. The words "remove all your clothes", the images from the pornographic magazine, no one home to help her, the feelings of fear, of being paralysed, flooding her mind like a download from the Matrix.

James only wanted the best for his wife, would support her no matter what she chose, but was moving back into the home where this traumatic experience had taken place the best thing for Annie?

Determined this past experience wasn't going to beat her, determined she was going to face up to it and move past it, just to see her dad smile and know the Montgomery family home was going to be in safe hands was the anchor Annie needed. She had James, and with him by her side, she could achieve anything.

With the deal done, the Davidson house packed up and the Montgomery home emptied, the Gibbins family moved home once more. Into the home where Annie's mother bullied her, her eldest brother raped her and where her middle brother was kidnapped. Was Annie just looking to torture herself? Or was this the only way she could move past it all, putting all the demons to rest?

Flashbacks of her being face down, face squashed into the pillow, her brother raping her, threats of exposing her with all the photos he'd forced her to take, calling her a fat slut, the extreme pain of him forcing himself into her, the 'click, click, click' of the camera, Annie knew she would never be able to enter *that* room in the property ever again. It would just be departmentalised, locked away in the recess of her mind, a part of the home which would be like a storage room, except instead of being stored full of boxes of family heirlooms and old family belongings, inside would be tragedy, trauma and betrayal.

With the house move complete and everything organised the way Annie wanted it, it was time to secure that CEO position for the Australasian Society for Ultrasound in Medicine (ASUM), a role in which she would remain in for five years, and of course thrive in. There she would meet Dr Sue Westerway, a woman who would go on to become a dear friend and confidante. Sue was President of ASUM at the time Annie was CEO, and they would share many triumphs, tribulations and a huge amount of fun along the way. Impressed by Annie's refreshing authenticity, and her deep heart felt desire to see other women achieve happiness, balance and success on their own terms, Sue reflected on her own journey of motherhood and balancing a career. Annie's adeptness to empower all those around her with her unique ability to unveil their true essence, whilst equipping them with the skills they needed to move forward in life, was something that constantly impressed Sue. Together they achieved a great many things, not just for ASUM, but for each other and those they worked with.

Under Annie's leadership the Society grew stronger and became a leader in the field of Ultrasound in the Australasian region, increasing awareness, updating the image and improving the transfer of knowledge both within the organisation and to those outside of it. Under her leadership, Annie had the pleasure of working with Ultrasound pioneers such as Dr William Garret, also known as Bill, a man who sadly passed away just before she stepped down as CEO and handed the reigns on.

He wasn't the only man to have passed away during the years Annie spent at the Society. Two years into her leadership at ASUM, her father was moved into a hospice where he spent the last month of his life. It didn't matter that Annie was CEO of a major national organisation, or that she had duties as a wife and mother to perform, she also had her duties as a daughter, to the man who had been her rock throughout her whole life. Throughout the entire month Mr Montgomery was in the hospice he had a lunch date with his beloved daughter, the one who he had seen rise to the very top of the business world, and prove to him she did indeed have the head for business, and a woman could run a business whilst having a family of not just the average 2.4 children, but five of them!

Although the journey had been much longer than the six to 12 months initially predicted by the doctors, he had been 'dying' for the entirety of his grandchildren's lives. Extremely sad, difficult and challenging it was, and a lingering worry in the back of the family's minds, but they had all pulled together, they had remained strong for each other, and it had made them all appreciate each other, and each moment they were given. Passing peacefully in his sleep was the blessing the family had hoped for, and the next morning the entire family were together to visit him one last time and say their farewells: a special moment never forgotten. Annie was completely heartbroken and did her best to not think about it, why would she want to make herself feel worse than she already did?

Living in the home where there were terrible memories, buying it to please her father, and now he wasn't here? Emotions of uncontrollable anger started to bubble, something Annie wasn't used to. Pushing people away, discovering the waves of grief swallowing her up, she was determined not to wallow in pain and despair. Thinking back to her lipstick moment back at Everest Base camp in Nepal and the concept she had used to start her own business Lipstick Consulting, was a saving grace many times over during those initial months after her dad died.

Still Annie showed up for work, still she showed up for her family, and still she did it with an elegance and a grace that had onlookers wonder where she got her impeccable strength and courage from. On the outside looking in, things were business as usual, driving forward with the Society, redecorating the family home to remove many of the memories and taking long walks and time by herself out into nature. Annie dug deep into prayer, allowed herself to be held by James, and crafted her Magic Transformation course for her business. She knew she wasn't the only woman who was trying to hold everything together. She knew she wasn't the only woman who needed a pick me up, and she knew so many women need to know they didn't have to 'do it' alone. She also knew it didn't matter how prepared or unprepared we think we are for times of struggle; those times can easily take you by surprise and reduce you to a mess on the floor.

As the months passed by, Annie learned healthy ways to move through the challenge, understanding on a much deeper level that adversity builds resilience. It wasn't just a quote thrown about by the personal development and self-help gurus, it was real. The rawness of emotion was real. The having it all together one moment and being a complete wreck the next was absolutely real, and it was this kind of life learning, which was now gripping her in its full power, that would help her curate a deeply magical, transformative programme for women. Her signature programme was being birthed, and although she didn't have all the finer details for it yet, she knew it was going to be one that helped other women to respond, cope and recover more effectively and efficiently in the future, in both their personal and professional lives.

But first she needed to remember to take time out to be, to feel, to process and to reset. She would be no good to anyone if she was tired, exhausted and not honouring herself.

With her first role of CEO going incredibly well, Annie was now a lot more confident in the belief she had always had higher level managerial skills, something the family still loved to laugh about together, Annie reminding the children, and James; with them all teasing her about it when the moment arose. Laughter and being playful was the medicine for so many of the various challenges the family had faced over the years, but so was gratitude for each other and all the blessings they had in life.

Time together, putting each other's best interests first and knowing that the best team is indeed family became even more important when in 2011 Annie received the news that her beloved grandma had passed away at the age of 99. Devastated at this sad news, Annie turned to her family for support and tapped into gratitude for having had such an incredible woman in her life, especially as a grandmother.

Later that year Annie and James took Hannah, Sam and Chelsea on a trip to Cambodia, Vietnam and Laos. A different kind of holiday lifestyle in comparison to the one Daniel and Caleb had, which consisted of thrifty farm holidays, with fish and chips and ice-cream, but it didn't matter, the boys loved those holidays, and they had the added bonus of having their mum home more than the younger three.

Having your mum around is something taken for granted by many and being shown life without parents is something the three youngest children were about to witness. For Annie and James, people who have such huge hearts, wanting to give back wasn't just about writing cheques, or doing a fundraiser. It was about rolling up your sleeves and getting stuck in, something the trip to would teach the youngest three children in abundance, especially as this 'holiday' was doing much needed work within the orphanages.

Caring for and playing with the orphans, showering them with love was no easy task for the family, especially knowing that they were there temporarily, and the moment they were gone the love and cuddles would disappear with them. The level of corruption within the orphanage networks in Cambodia means many of the toys donated are taken to the markets as soon as the guests have left and sold to line the pockets of directors of the orphanages. Many of the children are starving, made to perform like circus monkeys on the streets for money, and then made to hand over the money passing tourists give them, otherwise they are beaten, made to starve even more, and in some cases raped from horrifically young ages.

Teaching English, completing some of the maintenance tasks and donating medical supplies was received with gratitude. With as much as 80% of Cambodian orphans being actors in a world of corruption, taken from their families at a young age to fund this sad and inhumane tourist theatre, it is the 20% of the orphans that truly need the love, joy and gifts that Annie, James and their much loved children gave so willingly. If it meant that they reached the hearts of just a handful of the children, changed their lives in some way for the better, then it was worth doing.

Challenged by what they saw and experienced, and overwhelmed by emotion, gratitude and love for each other, the family headed back to Australia very different people. They couldn't allow themselves to get drawn into what may or may not be true, they simply had to focus on the fact that those children needed love, joy and attention, and that is what each one of them had given, without agenda, without ego, just open hearted warmth and love.

It was in 2014 that this family team would be tested again in a variety of ways, starting with the anniversary of Annie's father's death. Always forgiving, always wanting to build bridges, Annie tried to make things better with her mum by going on a trip with her. Thinking it would be a nice idea for her mum to go back to France and retrace her childhood roots, a place she lived until she was 12, reconnect with some old family friends and then take a river cruise from Amsterdam to Budapest, the trip was agreed to and Annie set about organising it. On the one condition stipulated by her mum, James had to go, not just Annie and her mum, but James too. With James booked to go on the trip too, and their youngest daughter Chelsea who was too young to leave at home, the foursome set off.

To everyone's surprise, locations and activities aside which they had no doubt would be amazing, it was a thoroughly enjoyable trip. They found both childhood homes, shared lots of wonderful memories and were on the river cruise in time for the anniversary of her father's passing away. Annie's mum was actually quite pleasant which was great, and Annie was really glad she'd made it happen, and that her mother could relax and enjoy this time together.

Having graduated from university with honours, Hannah secured a teaching job straightaway and absolutely loved it. Sadly though, the huge amount of work and pressure upon the teachers, in addition to feeling that teaching wasn't her true passion, led to a level of overwhelm which was just too much for her to handle. Terrified that she would return back to her previous levels of anxiety and depression, Hannah confided in her mum and told her that after three years of teaching full-time she didn't want to go back to work as a teacher. After all the initial hugs, and tears from Hannah, Annie and James sat down with her and discussed all the options. They both knew how intense the workload could be due to their own work in the teaching profession. They did their best to reassure Hannah that it was going to get easier, and she should really consider staying, especially as it was a safe job to have, but it was too late. Hannah's mind was made up.

Feeling as though she had let herself and her parents down, especially now as her mum's eyes would sparkle with pride at the success of

Hannah's older brother Caleb who was doing so well at university studying Law, Hannah's depression returned with vengeance.

Wanting what was best for their daughter, both Annie and James told her that it didn't matter what job she did, the most important thing was she was happy. Over a discussion between James and Annie it was decided that Annie would take Hannah away for a few days during the school holidays; have some Mama-Daughter time in Bateman's Bay, and visit the privately owned Mogo Zoo. With the zoo dedicated to the conservation of endangered animals, there was plenty to boost both women's spirits.

Opened in 1991 the zoo has around 221 animals across 42 species. One of the best moments of this trip, other than having her mum all to herself, was Hannah got to hold, see and get up close and personal with a red panda, her all-time favourite animal. Having this downtime together away from the world was just what both of them needed. A bond already strong was strengthened and the feelings of being so incredibly blessed to have each other caused many a tear to be shed, mostly by Hannah, but who was counting? All that mattered was the feelings of shame and guilt, feeling like she 'should be stronger' and 'was a disappointment to her parents', had disappeared and Hannah was smiling again.

Back home and after many years of gentle hiking, Annie's mind was ticking over, and over many coffees, tipsy evenings with her dearest friend Ilda, it was decided that a challenge was in order. It was agreed they would both enter the premier hiking challenge for women named Coastrek, organised by an Australian based organisation called Wild Women on Top. Both ladies were keen hikers and wanted to push themselves further than they had before, and being ladies who didn't hang about, or cut corners, they got straight into training.

Be kind and be generous in all that you do

Chapter Nineteen

BECOMING A PHILANTHROPIST

With the boot laces done up and all the preparations completed, it was time for their first attempt at a major hike. Taking part in the 2014 Sydney Coastrek event, the same year the organisation launched their 30-60 kilometres Team Trekking Challenge, was going to be the start of annual fundraising events for Annie. It wasn't going to be an easy hike either, taking the friends 15 hours to complete. Still, plenty of time for a great natter, a bloody good giggle and a walk along 60 kilometre of the most breath-taking paths the region has to offer.

Many people had nervously laughed off their own ability to take part in such an event, but now the children were more independent, Annie had more time for herself and wasn't 'just' a mum anymore. Both sets of twins had finished school, Chelsea was on the home straight and so there was more time to become even more of the woman she was born to be. Plus, Annie had a plan to live a very long time, so she had better keep her mind, body and spirit in great shape, not to mention make sure this long life she had planned was of continued great quality.

Getting through the 60 kilometres was a great achievement, especially considering Annie had raised $2000 AUD for the Fred Hollows Foundation[1] which was founded in 1992 by eye surgeon Fred Hollows shortly before he died. Hollows was an incredibly talented surgeon, a social justice activist who was committed to improving eye health for Aboriginals, and for those in developing countries such as Eritrea, Nepal and Vietnam, as well as an instigator of bringing down the cost of eye health care and educating the Indigenous population of all the 19 countries his foundation now operates in, thanks to his widowed wife Gabby carrying out his work after his death.

Coastrek[2] had been organising events since 2009 so had a growing number of participants. Having enjoyed the trek so much in 2014, Annie registered again for 2015, this time convincing daughter Hannah to join her and Ilda. Although not as eager to walk the 60 kilometres as her mum was, Hannah agreed and started training.

As the year passed on by, Annie and Ilda got together with a group of ladies in the Northern Beaches area, ones they had become friends with from the Wild Women on Top treks, and started to increase their training to two to three hours a day. With endless positive energy and a ready for anything attitude, both friends became more like sisters to one another. One of the character traits Ilda came to admire and deeply respect about Annie was that it didn't matter who she was with, or who was around her, she was always Annie. No pretence, no hiding who she was, she was just simply Annie, a rare gem with a brain that is always ticking with ideas, not failing to mention a laugh which lifts the hearts and spirits of everyone around. Annie's kind and caring nature, topped off with straight talking and an incredible sense of humour made everyone warm to her, want to be around her, and feel comfortable in her presence. A rare gem indeed for women in business, and one's who had achieved the level of success Annie had achieved.

The time was edging ever closer and Hannah was getting really nervous about completing the trek from Palm Beach, the location for Australia's greatest TV export 'Home and Away' all the way to Balmoral. Having inherited her mother's determination and strength, albeit in a different way, and knowing her mum would be with her, Hannah rose to the occasion and completed the walk. It wasn't without some interesting twists and turns along the way though. Suffering pain from badly blistered feet and the realisation that the finish line was not too far away, there was still a mountain to climb; a great metaphor for life if ever there was one! Having walked the Coastrek with her mum and a great group of ladies, all of whom continually supported and encouraged each other, Hannah knew for certain this was the one and only time she would be taking part. Annie being super fit at this point, and no longer suffering from her life-threatening asthma attacks, took turns being up front in the lead to hanging back and supporting those who really needed it.

Having completed the Sydney Coastrek, and raising $5000 in the process, Annie had her next adventure with Ilda to look forward to. This time she was off to Nepal with Ilda to trek to Ama Dablam Base Camp. With the 'warm up' along the coast in Sydney completed it was time to head 14,993 feet above sea level, to the base camp situated 4,570 metres up in the mountains. These may have been a very different kind of mountain to the one Hannah climbed with her mum on the Coastrek, but everything is relative, and a mountain is still a mountain depending on your perspective. Designed to take trekkers through the various Sherpa villages Ama Dablam, meaning 'mother's necklace' due to the way the hanging glaciers resemble the traditional jewellery worn for centuries by the Sherpa women, follows the same trail for many of the other trails on the way to Everest Base Camp, and beyond.

Joining other trekkers, the ladies were all set to go and have the adventure of a lifetime. With photos taken at various intervals of the breath-taking scenery, Annie and Ilda had a truly amazing time in some of the most rugged landscapes on the planet. Although Annie's asthma had been the thing to take away Annie's breath over the years, this time not even the high altitude and lack of oxygen could compete with the sun shining on snowy peaks, the incredible blue skies and the vastness of it all. Even though both Annie and James were in Nepal at the same time, James was deep in his purpose of giving back and helping others on an optical aid trip. Both with great photos, just of different aspects of the country, and capturing very different energy levels.

Returning home with enough photos taken to make even a snap happy tourist jealous, Annie couldn't wait to share her awe-inspiring journey with James. Filled with laughter, a deepened friendship with Ilda and exciting memories, Annie had trouble even keeping up with her own pace of retelling the story. There was so much to share, so much to say, and the only way James was going to overcome the hit of loving jealousy was to ask his beautiful wife to take him back the following year, but this time to do Everest Base Camp together. Annie pondered on the idea for all of a millisecond before agreeing and nearly blowing her own record for levels of excitement in any one person.

His wife may be the most insanely energetic woman he had ever met, but after all the years they had spent together, James couldn't look at his high speed animated wife radiate with joy and not fall deeper in love with her. Often, he would find himself watching her give a speech, such as the one she did for Mother's Day at their local church and find himself bursting with pride. Watching her in full on 'Annie Mode' and knowing she too had an immense crush on him often surprised him. Was he really that lucky? A wife who not only blew his socks off with her endless energy, constantly hyperactive mind, but also a woman who just wanted to support others to be the best version of themselves, to help make a positive difference in the lives of others, giving back whenever she could, to see someone smile, or feel better about themselves.

The times he had seen her speaking at conferences, being the MC at events such as the Annual Ultrasound Dinner, watching how others would hang on her every word, he would feel incredibly proud of all she had achieved. To have a guy sat next to him nudge him and tell him he was a lucky guy to be married to such a beautiful woman, yeah, he was a lucky guy. They had both been through so much together, and they were stronger now than they had ever been.

The thing was though, Annie felt the exact same way about James. Through supporting each other, and others, giving their attention to the things that mattered to them and to others, being in a constant state of gratitude, had allowed them to live an incredible life together; and both of them were still only just getting started!

---

1. https://www.hollows.org/au/home
2. https://www.coastrek.com.au/

It only seems impossible until you find a way

Chapter Twenty
BECOMING INNOVATIVE

As 2016 rolled around, James was becoming frustrated with the way things were going with his role at TAFE. He had been a lecturer there for well over a decade and he was no longer feeling fulfilled or challenged. One night whilst sharing with Annie his thoughts and feelings, Annie surprised him by asking, "Why don't you just start your own college?"

For Annie this was just the next natural step to take, but was going up against the Australian government really the right move to make? It was a bold move if it was anything, but with Annie's encouragement, her total love and support, he knew he could do it. He had the skills, the experience, the network, and the ideas, the only thing stopping him was handing in his resignation and going for it. The family foundation was strong, so taking this kind of perceived risk was not an issue. They were both safe to build upon what many would think was a dangerous move, and with Annie's fiercely competitive nature, combined with everything they had learnt on their respective journeys, they were more than ready to take on the challenge. Two huge challenges set for the year, and with Annie and James being the emerging power couple to take notice of, there was no doubt both the challenges would succeed, and if a third or fourth appeared, then they would just deal with those in the only way they knew how, the positive way.

With Annie being the catalyst behind setting up the Australasian College of Optical Dispensing, and James happy to admit that without her by his side, he would never have had the courage to go for it –

something echoed by their eldest son Caleb – it seemed there were no limits on what can be achieved with a large dose of curiosity and drive for positively impacting people's lives.

Returning to the family home for visits, their eldest son Caleb noticed how life was changing for the better, not just financially, but also in the endless energy his parents seemed to be gaining. His mum looked better than she had ever done and when most women her age would be slowing down, his mum was accelerating, something he finds both impressive and admirable in his mum. Her evolution and pace of development, her commitment to herself and others didn't stop. Her move from public to private sector as CEO was the next big step for Annie, and although the sector changed the subject matter didn't.

The Australian Institute of Ultrasound, a leader in its field for 21 years already was looking for someone to move them even further ahead in their field of providing hands-on, practical ultrasound training. It seemed Annie's love affair with teaching and improving people's lives would be reaching a whole new audience and using the latest in advanced equipment to deliver the very best in both hands-on and theoretical training.

With a trip to Nepal planned in October to meet with Dr Gentle Shrestha and Professor Marhatta, Head of Anaesthesiology of Tribhuvan University Teaching Hospital, it would be a great idea to combine this trip with her Everest Base Camp adventure with James.

There would be enough time with everything going on of course to take in another successful year of fundraising with the Wild Women on Top on their annual Coastrek. This year Annie would complete the 60 kilometre trek in Melbourne, beating her personal best fundraising with a grand total of $5348. Wanting to push her fundraising target further and raise awareness of the level of poverty she had been witnessing around the country due to her work in healthcare. Knowing poverty wasn't just about low level income, but also about low level health, especially for those on the streets, Annie's ever giving heart had her enrol in the CEO Sleep Out[1] which was helping to fund the St Vincent de Paul Society[2].

With the date set, Annie got to work, started promoting the event and the causes involved, raising another $5000 for charity. Annie's work wasn't about looking good in the boardroom, or treading on people to get to the top, nor was it about putting other people down, it was about celebrating people in all their greatness, no matter how great they saw themselves, she always managed to make them feel greater about themselves.

With his mother's rise to success, Caleb was watching with great fascination, and not just from the business angle. He was observing the 'Tall Poppy Syndrome' which is sadly very common the world over, especially amongst women; something Annie would be on the receiving end the more she went after her next big challenges, because Annie being Annie, there was never 'just another one' around the corner.

Caleb also noticed with interest how people changed towards the family, not just in person but on social media as a whole. Those who had only known Annie for a short time celebrated her and those who had known her for as long as Caleb could remember were either nowhere to be seen, or slow at coming forward; leading him to realise that you can't be successful or famous in your home town, well not until you've *really* made it. Caleb realised this is a global phenomenon and sadly one of the things that puts a lot of distance between friends as one rises in their chosen career paths. Caleb, very much like his mother, was watching and learning fast, and setting himself up to launch his own investment company, a company which would revolutionise the way parents invested money for, and with, their children.

As the year progressed, so did James' new business venture, and the training for Everest Base Camp. Soon James would get to experience the awe and the conditions Annie was so excited about a year before, and Annie would experience yet another defining moment in her life. Months of fitness training prepared them to push their bodies to the limit as they enjoyed the incredible surrounds of the most remote and wild places on the planet. The challenge of hiking in snow at altitude while head to toe in waterproof gear for 21 days was a great way to test her comfort zone when stripped of life comforts and dreaming of a shower, electric blanket, glass of wine and cheese. The trek proved challenging for a woman previously not known for her sporting prowess, but then again being presented with two sets of twins and the possibility of triplets back in the start of her parenting journey, Base Camp was just another opportunity to show how raw grit and determination can make the seemingly impossible possible.

One night whilst heading down to the mess tent for dinner, having been trekking all day, Annie turned to her beloved James and said, 'hold on, I just want to put on my lippy.' James has grown used to Annie's crazy ideas over the years, but this time he gave her this weird look as if to say, 'Are you suffering altitude sickness?'. With a mix of concern and bewilderment James replied, 'But you don't need it. Why bother, no-one here cares if you have lipstick on'. In quick response Annie came back with, 'I care!' so James waited, Annie applied her lipstick, and she instantly felt better about herself, even though she hadn't washed for two weeks!! It was this moment which caused Annie to reflect on things over the next few weeks, but in the meantime, it was time for dinner, and after a day of trekking, dinner was much needed.

The next day as Annie climbed another mountain, through another snowdrift, sucking in the air at high altitude, she thought back to that simple act of applying lipstick. For some reason it was causing her to reflect on her next career move and question her purpose and passion. It was then she chose to become an entrepreneur and start her own company. It was an opportunity to grow something pure, and true to herself that she could then use to empower and support women around the world. It would still be running a company, but this time it would be without the foundations being laid by others, it would be her and her alone building the foundations of a business and growing it. She would be following not only in her father's footsteps of buying and building the pharmacy, but also being a pioneering woman like her beloved grandmothers.

Back on Australian soil, and work underway to develop Lipstick Consulting, the name for her new business, Annie's curious mind started wandering again. Having moved over into the private sector of ultrasound medicine, Annie was seeing a whole new way of doing business, and it excited her. A lot. Combining both her own and James' knowledge they were coming up with some incredibly strong propositions for the Australasian College of Optical Dispensing. They would certainly be giving TAFE a run for its money, that's for sure. Being a privately run college, there was a lot more freedom to invest, innovate and lead, and the couple were now really making their mark in the Australian world of medicine. Highly respected before, but now with this big bold move of going up against TAFE, they had opened eyes and doors previously closed, and with these openings, Annie's curiosity got even more curious about what was truly possible.

What was it that really drove this woman, and did she actually know what it meant to have an uncomfortable zone? It didn't matter what Annie did, there was always more to do. More heart centred service to others, more adventures with those she loved, more laughter to be had, and certainly more conversations, something Annie never ran short of.

Being able to chatter away at high speed was a skill few others seemed to possess, and the thing was, it wasn't mindless chatter. It was always with the intention to speak kindly, to be playful, to spread joy and to discuss ideas. Not just ideas for dinner, although food still played a big part in Annie's life, this time with a much healthier balance and focus. The ideas Annie was having were surprising, inspiring and always exciting, whether an exciting business idea or an exciting night out with the girls celebrating with champagne. This excitement benefitted everyone, and although Annie had a fiery, no nonsense approach to getting things done, she had an incredible way of reducing the clinical feel to many of the industries she entered, none more so with her migration into the optical health market.

When she wasn't helping James with the college project, or dealing with her CEO duties for the institute, she was developing her business model for Lipstick Consulting, and her Magic Transformation Programmes. With so many transformational programmes on the market, she had to make it different. She had to make it stand out from the crowd in true Annie Gibbins fashion, and it had to have a real sense of adventure and curiosity about it. With the ideas starting to form in her mind in a much more crystallised fashion, knowing she had everything it took to bring out the very best out of women, her fully online Business and Life modules would be designed to bring out each woman's unique abilities as well as the team spirit in each and every woman who took part. Now all she had to do was bring it to market.

The fun, healthy competition between husband and wife would prove to be an immense blessing, with everything an opportunity rather than an obstacle. A few would have their doubts about Annie entering this new market with James, but as always, Annie knew how to arrive on the scene and she knew how to win people over from a place of genuine interest and serving the wider community in the best possible way.

---

1. https://www.ceosleepout.org.au/
2. https://www.vinnies.org.au/

Always pushing boundaries. What's next?

Chapter Twenty-One
BECOMING AUDACIOUS

Daily fitness, ongoing giggles and making sure she looked great from the inside out were non-negotiables for Annie. It wasn't enough to dress well and have her nails done. Eating well, prayer and gratitude all went towards that radiant glow that shone from her eyes as well as her beautiful smile. Making sure she continued to invest in her knowledge, professional growth and her community, was more important than ever. She was about to enter a new sector of the medical world, and a new network of people now she was co-director of James' new venture.

As with all transitions from one sector to another, one job role to another, there would be people who would have their doubts about Annie due to her lack of experience in the eye health market, but focusing on that wasn't even on Annie's radar. Her laser focus, sharp mind and pure intentions would disperse all and every doubt anyone could come up with, all the doubters had to do was be ready for a dose of Annie.

With the 2017 60 kilometres Coastrek coming up on the Sunshine Coast, the regular training sessions Annie was doing was helping focus her mind on all areas of life. There was a lot to do and taking a breather from working the mind to working the body allowed the power of physiology to take over.

For years we have all been told that mind, body and soul when used together creates positive results, and Annie is living proof of this. Her mind was also ticking over, and even when climbing rock faces or trekking through the mountains there was always a curiosity about what was next? What is possible now I have achieved this? The excitement would build, and the heart would fill up with gratitude for all she was achieving in that very moment. Having an attitude of gratitude and being in the moment invigorated Annie in every cell of her body. Endorphins rushed and serotonin would increase, no wonder Annie was always so full of energy!

Over the years a few people had made her life unpleasant, others had fallen by the wayside, but there was one person in particular that Annie had yet to make peace with, and that was her mum. Annie and her mum had enjoyed each other's company on the anniversary of the death of Annie's father, but there was still a lot of ill-feeling between them. The situation needed dealing with after having been in therapy for what would be 20 years resolving this issue and any other challenges that came up.

The philosophy of 'take something good and make it great' hadn't changed since James and Annie had taken marriage guidance together before they were even married. Now with all the knowledge and personal development over the years, Annie had been able to use a lot of the personal development and coaching practices on herself. Starting with herself was always a great way of tackling any situation. "Where can I be responsible for the things I can control?" would always be one of the first questions Annie would ask, and one of the things she could control was putting one foot in front of the other and joining her ladies for some fun and laughter whilst raising yet another $2000 for the Fred Hollows Foundation.

Being involved with supporting the foundation, Annie was learning more and more about eye health, and combined with the things she had learnt via James over the years, and now being director of the Australasian College of Optical Dispensing, it was not surprising Annie was now keeping a closer eye on the developments within the industry.

Plus, she was looking for another new challenge and true to her very own saying 'Do things when you are ready, and believe this is the best day ever, every day' she kept her eyes and ears open looking for the next opportunity to grow and create a ripple effect of positive impact in the world.

One of the best days of the year was when Caleb and Beth announced the news that they were expecting their first child together.

Squeals of delight, hands to her face in a wave of wonderful emotion, realising a new Gibbins was joining the family, and that she and James were about to become grandparents was a heart-warming moment Annie will never forget, especially as James was on the brink of happy tears before Annie.

Samuel was also in love with Alice and all things on the family frontier was evolving as fast as Annie was, or it was calling her forward into her next level of life. Hannah was flourishing in University, Daniel and Chelsea were happy doing their thing and life was great, and again, it was only about to get better!

Looking at her past experience and all she had achieved thus far, Annie started to prepare for her next transition and applied for a new CEO position. There was some tough competition, but Annie was competitive, and Annie was focused, and she wanted the role she was applying for. With ideas already cascading through her mind, lipstick applied and game face on, it was time to enter the process of application for her new role as CEO of Glaucoma Australia, succeeding Geoff Pollard who was going into retirement after seven years at the helm.

Bringing over 15 years of senior management experience to Glaucoma Australia's mission of eliminating glaucoma blindness, a challenge in itself, Annie was chosen from a really tough selection process from a strong group of candidates. Mr Ron Spithill OAM, the President of Glaucoma Australia had commended the then current CEO Mr Geoff Pollard on his outstanding contribution. Knowing Mr Pollard was leaving Glaucoma Australia in a stronger position than any other time in its almost 30-year history, it was time for Annie to make it even stronger, forge ahead as a leader in its field and create a "powerful force for change in the war against the blinding impact of glaucoma", to use Mr Spithill's words in his welcoming speech.

Looking at the organisation through the eyes of a patient, family member, a member of the public and a training provider for medical specialists and nurses, Annie set to work. One of the first things to get sorted was the new branding, and a new tagline, which after some thought and discussion with team members, 'Saving Sight' emerged alongside the new risk awareness campaign, designed to create greater awareness of the broad range of glaucoma risk factors. It didn't take

Annie and her team long and within the first six months all these changes were implemented, not to mention the new and improved digital referral systems.

Her attention then turned to supporters of the organisation and how patients, carers and nurses could access the information for free. It was time to gift knowledge and bring on some champions such as the Governor General of Australia and Kirk Pengilly from INXS, finding companies and individuals who would fund and champion the work Glaucoma Australia did. With a clear vision of the road ahead, Annie started making a list of people who she wanted support from.

Being a little bit cheeky, and with a boldness unknown by a woman in the industry before, Annie would giggle to herself wondering, *What do I need to do to get a 'Yes!' from these people?* With a list of names and knowing the public and private sector needed to take a few more risks, it was time to put some appropriate stretching in place. Some people within the organisation may have been panicking and thinking Annie was punching way above her weight. But Annie knew that unless we expect more from ourselves and our organisations, then we are never going to achieve more.

When Annie started in her role as CEO she was given four strategy pillars which gave a directional framework, but without a real plan of how that was used to solve the complex problem, Annie started dreaming up a plan, designed it and then brought it into reality. Knowing that 50% of people with glaucoma are currently undiagnosed, which meant losing their sight was preventable, and 50% who are diagnosed were unintentionally losing their sight due to a number of factors, Annie knew there was no time to waste and put her high levels of energy to great use.

She kept thinking back to the decline in her dad's health with the brain tumour, the frustrations, the ideas and the insights and the blockages to treatment and knowledge. Knowing there was only 300 referrals annually didn't make sense with all Annie had learnt over the years with James' career. People didn't know enough about what was on offer, both the public and the optical industry, nor did they know how the impact of the problems of glaucoma were being measured at specific stages of their journey.

Looking at how she had measured her own success in all areas of life from her own education, the fitness training for the treks around New South Wales and Nepal, Annie knew how to listen to her body and track the process. Being great at communication, both at speaking and listening, Annie realised Glaucoma Australia needed to communicate better the benefits of early detection to patients and eye health professional to encourage referrals. Doing this would mean saving the eyesight of so many more people and giving them back their independence.

With all the changes and implementations Annie was making, and the industry feedback she received, she went on to secure a Platinum Sponsor. A younger demographic now felt comfortable reaching out and those who had believed Glaucoma was an 'old people's thing' were now getting the support they needed. They were no longer an old people's organisation. The Board of Glaucoma brought on a new President Associate Professor Simon Skalicky, amongst others, and the image of the organisation was changing and changing fast. Being a firm believer in education and taking things to the next level, Annie was instrumental in making sure the new Board members had Company Director qualifications to ensure a higher level of governance moving forward.

With the new Saving Sight campaign Annie introduced the average age of referrals dropped from 80-89 to 60-69. Knowing that every day she was making a positive difference to people's lives, and in this case saving sight, was a pretty awesome feeling for Annie. Being a woman who was instrumental in bringing about such a significant change shouldn't have been a big deal, but it was, and still is today. Annie knew that women have a long way to achieve equality and was determined to keep thriving and playing her part in changing the way women are seen in the industry, and business as a whole. Knowing how her grandma and mama had thrived and been pioneering women in such difficult times was a lot of comfort to Annie. Knowing they were both looking down on her from heaven and wearing her grandma's ring as a totem to be mindful and keep believing in herself, was of great comfort to Annie.

Creating such incredible results in such a short space of time, Annie was muscling in on some pretty big conversations being had within the industry. People were wanting to know what she thought and being an extraordinary bundle of energy and positivity Annie was proving she had an incredible way of getting content out of people to promote an array of subjects via press-releases, speeches and interviews. It helped that there was no stand-offish arrogance about her, and when Annie met Melanie Kell, the editor of *MiVision* magazine, the amount of content Annie provided Melanie with, they were getting the messages out there that needed to be heard. The tide was turning, and more and more women were coming into the industry, sparking a whole new level of energy which meant great change was looming. There had been very few women in the world of eye health that had made a difference, and none quite so as enthusiastic as Annie.

Failure provides the ultimate opportunity to learn, grow and change

Chapter Twenty-Two

BECOMING WISER

Life outside of the boardroom of Glaucoma Australia was also going through its own transformation. James was taking the educational market by storm and becoming even more playfully competitive with his wife.

When Annie applied for a job in 'his industry' he knew things would become a lot more fun for the both of them. Now they were speaking at the same events, sat in audiences together, watching each other shine, working together on their very own business, he got to see a whole new side of this woman he got to call his wife. He was seeing her higher-level managerial skills play out and he was bursting with pride as her contribution to an industry he had spent his entire working life working in. He didn't think it was possible to fall in love with her even more, but that is what was happening.

Sharing stages with inspirational leaders such as Stephen De Sede, founder of the De Sede Institute; Aldo Grech, Environmentalist, Inventor and Feminist, and leading ophthalmic surgeons and optometric academics, Annie inspired change just by being who she was. With no ego, a gorgeous smile and a purpose to make everyone believe in themselves, it was hard for the Australian market to not stand back and take notice of what Annie had to say. Simply by sharing who she was, her thoughts and ideas, with the passion she had for giving back and living the best life for as long as possible, Annie was transforming lives all around the world.

Whilst climbing with her soul sister and best friend Ilda during 2018, Annie sprung into Nurse Annie mode when a man with a head injury needed support. When the mountain rescue team arrived, they couldn't help but admire the skills, calm nature and presence Annie had, and the peace she had brought to a complete stranger.

With her unpredictable and beautiful mind, always up for an adventure, Annie organised a three-day camping trip with the Australian School of Mountaineering, taking Ilda and a few other women with her.

At 2228 metres above sea level, Mount Kosciuszko, Australia's highest mountain, Annie and Ilda were met with a blizzard, one that reduced visibility to just a few metres.

Now being an experienced climber and trekker, Ilda had no doubts she and the other campers were in safe hands. Always making sure everyone was okay, and with positivity and a vibrancy that was both encouraging and motivating, Annie took her campers on a walk in the blizzard, giving them the best experience of their lives, and a much needed hot chocolate at the other end. All for an extra bit of spice and celebration, Annie enjoyed her favourite Peach Schnapps at the Eagles Nest Pub and was keen to eat a proper meal because although a lover of the great outdoors, Annie was not a fan of camping food.

Bringing out the very best in people, gifting them their greatest memories, whilst showing Ilda and the other campers that the strength they admired and appreciated in nature was deep within themselves, gave everyone a confidence like never before. It was just the 'Annie way', and one of the many reasons why so many people when working with her felt they could achieve anything.

Understanding the learning is never done, and that everyone is a teacher, is one of the key secrets to Annie's success, along with the fact that she allowed herself to be coachable, is always investing in herself and her future. Whilst most women 'her age' are slowing down, Annie is just getting started, and showcasing what it is really like to be fifty years of age.

Defying the ageing process with her inner peace, her positive attitude, love of giving back to society, and her rule breaking, there is no wonder the people who know Annie either up close and personal or from a distance are so in love with who she is. She is living proof that you don't have to look tired and run down at fifty, you don't 'just have to be a housewife' and you don't 'have to slow down'. The phrase goes that life begins at forty, but Annie is smashing that phrase and proving that life can start at any age, all you have to do is choose to be who you are, set an intention and take action.

With colleagues such as Stephen De Sede referring to Annie's 'gifted soul' combined with her ambition and desire to be fulfilled is what makes her one of the most attractive leaders for both men and women in the world today, Annie's gratitude and humility makes sure she reflects this back out into the world echoing it for others so they too believe they are capable of all they wish and get curious and ambitious about.

With her elegant rise to the top, Annie knew that there were still things hiding in the shadows of her life which needed dealing with. Her relationship with her mother for one, and finally releasing herself from the weight on her shoulders which was still holding her back in a number of ways; although knowing Annie, no one could honestly say there was anything holding her back. A few women in her space were intimidated by her and all she managed to achieve in a day, and still look amazing whilst doing it.

Telling her mum about what happened with her brother was no easy task, but sharing it gave Annie space in her heart and mind to fill with peace, relief and love for herself. This wasn't her burden to carry, this was not her stuff to hold onto any longer, and so sharing with her mum why she had not wanted to be around her brother, protecting her children from him, and explaining why she had been the way she had was much needed.

Of course, her mum didn't believe her – called her a liar – and, who can blame her? What mother would want to hear this from her daughter about her own son? How could she even begin to process all of this? So, Annie booked them into a therapy session together, it was something they had to unravel together, and with her mum getting older, Annie wanted peace between them.

Sadly, this was not to be the case as during the consultation her mum shouted insults, accusing Annie of all kinds of things, before eventually refusing to acknowledge she has a daughter. Letting go of this relationship with her mother was a hard choice, an extremely sad choice but necessary. She was a lamb to the slaughter no more.

Facing up to the challenges and the memories was only one part of the journey to releasing herself from her past. There was still the issue of how she kept avoiding the room in the family home. Telling herself she could deal with it and move past it would keep her focused on the family, her work with James and with Glaucoma Australia. Becoming at peace with her brother's failure in morality and protecting his younger sister made her stronger and wiser, a better mother, and knew that now she had taken these powerful steps, she would be able to embrace change on a whole new level, it is after all what she helped the women do on her Magic Transformation Programme, which she was now delivering to women around the world under her very own company Lipstick Consulting.

2018 was one of the most momentous years so far in Annie's life. Not only would she become a grandmother for the very first time, something both she and James were incredibly excited about, but she would also embark on a 16-week course to develop and elevate the brand for Lipstick Consulting. Of course, this was something Annie would excel at, little did she know though she would go on to become the best student the course leader had ever had.

Always on a mission, showcasing what it was like to be on natural speed as she built her digital assets, Annie was enjoying the opportunity to create and build the stepping stones to expand her consultancy business, as well as use the knowledge to accelerate the Australasian College of Optical Dispensing, as well as Glaucoma Australia.

By week 14 of the 16 week course, Annie had not only set a whole new standard in the history of the course she attended, but she had also sold 30 places on her Magic Transformation course, changing the lives of not just 30 women, but the lives of all the people these magical women came into contact with.

With that achievement under her belt, it was time for Annie to take part in her fifth Coastrek event, this time in Adelaide. It was another 60 kilometre trek and another $2000 to add to the total she had already raised to help save the eyesight and independence of people in Australasia and Asia. Having completed the Coastrek for five years running now, Annie was becoming a familiar face amongst the diehard trekkers. Her infectious giggle and friendly nature inspired those who met her the first time to sign up again the next year, joining the family of

Wild Women and making friends who they would never normally have met.

One of the things Annie loved about taking part in events like Coastrek was the camaraderie, encouragement and sisterhood that took place. Women working together for the sake of something greater than themselves, something that was still very much needed in the world of work. With women in her space still feeling threatened by another woman's success, or how attractive they were, she navigated the backbiting and friendships lost along the way, not to mention a lot of opportunities to make the world a better place.

Being a heart warrior, a name given to her by one of her mentors Stephen De Sede, Annie would offer pro-bono and discounted mentoring to a wide range of ladies for a host of different reasons. For all those who wanted to take part in her Magic Transformation Program, there was an opportunity to apply for a scholarship. Impacting lives was not just about charity, nor was it always about discounting, or gifting scholarships to people, but it was about making them see that more they invested in themselves, the more opportunities would open up to them.

Annie had invested heavily in her education, her physical, emotional and energetic development, and it had not always been easy. Sometimes the thought of investing a certain amount of money in her education would mean getting uncomfortable, but looking at the opportunities of getting to know more about what was possible, meeting others on the program or in the network of people associated with the coach or mentor, the impact she could then go on to create in the world, would always mean the investment was worth it, and what is life about if we don't get uncomfortable and choose to excel at being who we are?

One of the many possibilities Annie was conjuring up in her forever ticking mind was the possibility of asking two particular men to join Glaucoma Australia. Kirk Pengilly, from the rock band INXS, one of Annie's favourites back in the day, had almost lost his sight at the age of 29 to acute angle closure glaucoma so it just made sense to Annie that of course he would want to become an Ambassador for the organisation. Why would he not want to? Operation Kirk Pengilly was underway!

The next gentleman Annie approached was His Excellency General the Honourable David Hurley AC DSC (Retd), Governor General. He wanted the very best for the citizens of Australia and surely joining forces with Annie and Glaucoma Australia would just make perfect sense to him, so again Annie set about finding out the other reasons he would want to say yes and got to work.

It would be almost another year until both men were on board and Annie would be standing proudly next to them both announcing their involvement with Glaucoma Australia, but once the deal was done it would mean many more speaking engagements, TV appearances and the start of something truly magical for the people who were under threat of losing their sight, not to mention their families and a great deal of satisfaction for all the scientists and medical professionals who were supported in their work by the organisation.

As the weeks and months ticked by Annie developed strong regard for Clinical Professor Ivan Goldberg founder of GA and now an honorary life member. His work had been ground-breaking, and not just in the scientific way either. His passion to share knowledge, regardless of subject matter, and his never-ending curiosity and love of an intellectual banquet was something both he and Annie had in common.

With the wedding of their youngest son Samuel fast approaching, and the birth of granddaughter Lizzie creating more excitement in the world of Annie, tears of gratitude were being shed at an alarming rate. How had this young girl who had been told she couldn't do so many things, now be at the top of corporate Australia, sitting on the couch next to a heart throb most women Annie's age would have pinned to their bedroom wall, and running not just one successful business but three, all fully supported by the love of an incredibly strong family and the hunkiest husband of them all (who still had to pinch himself because he was the lucky guy his amazing woman had chosen to have the most insane life adventure with!).

And the journey of Annie was not over yet. There was still a lot more work to be done, another Coastrek to do, this time the 60 kilometre trek in Melbourne, raising another $2000 for the Fred Hollows Foundation, bringing the grand total to $17,000 since she first started doing the Coastrek events in 2014.

Launching her very own podcast, *Memoirs of Successful Women*, highlighting successful women around the world was going to be next on her list of achievements and meant that Annie got to celebrate other women doing incredible things, and being leaders for so many other women who needed the inspiration she had gained from her grandmothers. With so many women being lone wolves in the world of business, or sacrificing their relationships or health for success, it seemed as though Annie had created a magical formula simply by being herself and simply by getting curious about what was truly possible in life when you did what you wanted and ignored negative commentary from other people. Listening to the negative chatter in your own mind can be deafening enough, without the negativity of other people. Trying to be all things to all people, whilst sacrificing yourself also doesn't work. Finding the balance of life, giving back and being grateful for everything you have and don't have in life, has been incredibly rewarding for Annie, and her family are the ones who have got to see the highs, lows, doubts and excitement from a front row seat.

With her higher-level managerial skills, humble leadership, constant chatter and excitement for life, Annie was noticed by yet another organisation in the medical world. An organisation which supports women around the world with the health of their uterus and chances of having children. It is a charity which is close to her heart for many reasons, and one that is also in total alignment with the work she does for women around the world. Celebrating women in all their shapes, sizes, abilities and capabilities is at the heart of what Annie does, so being invited to join the board of **MRKH**[1] Australia in June 2020 was simply the icing on a very beautiful cake that Annie has discovered the ingredients for whilst on her magical mystery tour of life. Providing education and support for all those affected by **MRKH**, including the medical professionals, and the friends and families of those who experience the condition, this organisation brings together Annie's lifetime of achievements in many ways, and allows her to keep fundraising[2] simply by being who she is.

And isn't that what we all want in life? To love what we do, whilst being all of who we are, and all of who we choose to be?

---

1. https://mrkhaustralia.org
2. https://www.mrkhaustralia.org/donate

I'm like a fine wine, improving with age

Chapter Twenty-Three

BECOMING REFLECTIVE

Dear Anne-Marie,

As you embark upon your journey into adulthood, I encourage you to trust your passionate heart and the deep truths it reveals to you.

You are already acutely aware of so many things that make you feel safe, secure and happy.

- The love you have for James
- The desire you have for a family of your own
- The goal you have of one day becoming a businesswoman
- The pure joy you feel when exploring natural landscapes and breathing fresh air
- The freedom you feel when not restricted by rules and beliefs which limit your potential to thrive in your circumstance
- The satisfaction you feel when helping others to be their best self or to brighten their day

Trust your instincts gorgeous girl, your heart is your compass and it desperately wants you to live a big bold life full of fun, adventure, challenge, growth and impact.

Resist wasting your time, energy and emotional stability on people who do not value your essence. They will suck the life out of you and cause you to stumble and fall.

As your curious mind eagerly asks, 'what if' and searches with an urgency to find 'what's next', try to balance your inquisitive nature and impatient disposition as there is enough time to do all that you desire.

The painful scars you carry from years gone by are deep but still raw and need professional help to set you free. In order to rewrite a healthy life narrative, you need help and support and lots of it. Those anchors need breaking and there is no better time than now to do this.

You were born to BE YOU which means you are quirky, curious, passionate, energetic and driven. These traits make you beautifully unique and there is no value in suppressing or resisting them. Those people who ask you to tone down and become more palatable are actually not your cup of tea and that's okay, they are not yours either.

I invite you to nurture your innate qualities by giving yourself permission to thrive. Start with self-love and self-care as these are essential before you attempt to love and care for anyone or anything else. Invest on your education and do that MBA you dream about! You are more than capable and let's face it, you don't want those higher-level managerial skills to go to waste!!

As you step into becoming Annie, I encourage you to embrace the many varied seasons which come from marriage, parenthood, friendships, personal and professional growth and treasure the special moments. These memories will bring abundant joy as you reminisce over the many years ahead and they are your gold nuggets.

If you follow your truth, proactively limit negative influences on your life and nurture a growth mindset, you have the ability to turn your wounds into superpowers. This is key to reaching your potential and then realising there are no limits to your future success, balance and happiness.

With all my love,

Annie xoxox

My heart is my compass and knows where my true purpose resides

Learn More About Annie

As you have read in the previous pages, Annie Gibbins is a formidable woman, and yet these pages still only show you part of this amazing lady.

You have learnt so much about Annie, and no doubt been impressed with her strength, courage and determination, her desire to serve others from her huge heart, leaving the world in a much better condition than how she found it at each stage of her journey.

Connecting with Annie via social media, joining her Magic Transformation Programme, and listening to the conversations on her *Memoirs of Successful Women* podcast you will see how this mum of twins twice over, adventurer and female influencer leads others to greatness by breaking all the rules of society in the best possible way.

You've read how she has achieved her Master of Education, Graduate Diploma of Education, Bachelor of Health Science Nursing, Lean Six Sigma, Cert III & IV Fitness and AICD, but these do not define her, or restrict her viewpoints.

Annie has a strong sense of strategic growth know-how and has implemented it across companies including Allergan, Pfizer, Toshiba, GE, Philips, Sonosite and Siemens; industry experience spans charities, associations, healthcare, education, non-profit, optical and technology.

She has 25+ years growing and transforming health and education businesses across Australasia. Is renowned by industry and peers for leading innovative health education transformation, dramatically enhancing stakeholder value and advancing scientific research. Annie is recognised by Boards for delivering major transformational and culture change across large, complex, customer-driven organisations, supported by strength in financial and operational management as well as business, workforce and asset management reform.

Annie partners with CEOs and boards in defining real challenges to business and developing solutions that embed long term sustainable operations. She specialises in removing core obstacles to growth including poor commercials return, inefficient and ineffective systems, disparate team focus and delivery.

All this knowledge, know-how and expertise, combined with her love of health, fitness and fundraising are at the heart the transformational work she does with women around the world.

You can find out more about Annie's Magic Transformation Programme by visiting https://anniegibbins.com/magictransformation

If you wish to book her as a speaker at your event, or a guest on your show, please visit www.anniegibbins.com for more details.

Author Profile

Born in the UK, Dawn Bates is best known for her profound wisdom, truth slaying and high energy, not to mention a trademark giggle which is as infectious as a flu epidemic.

As well as being an international bestselling author, ghost writer and author coach, Dawn is an online entrepreneur, specialising in developing step change strategies and global visions, underpinned with powerful leadership and profound truths.

She writes for various global magazines, and when not sailing around the world on yachts, she appears on various media channels highlighting and discussing important subjects in today's society.

Dawn's first trilogy *The Trilogy of Life Itself* is powerful. It brings together the multi-faceted aspects of the world we live in and takes you on a rollercoaster ride that will leave you wanting more from life. A body of work that captures life around the world from the last 30 years, it is a time capsule that inspires, motivates and empowers all who read it.

Having worked in the field of female leadership, cultural diversity and community regeneration for the past 22 years, Dawn's expertise lies in making you rethink your life and the world we live in. She's an authority on leading others to create exceptional results, shifting all those who work with her from emotions such as fear, feelings of imposter and self-doubt to living life where they are free to speak their truth without guilt, shame and hesitation.

To discover more about how to work with Dawn, to book her as a speaker at your event, or a guest on your show please visit www.dawnbates.com.

www.ingramcontent.com/pod-product-compliance
Lightning Source LLC
Chambersburg PA
CBHW030437010526
44118CB00011B/675